Carving &
GREEN-WINGED TEAL
with Jim Sprankle

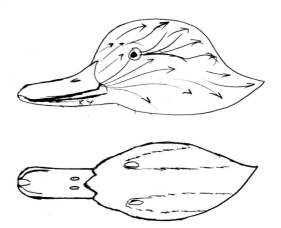

Curtis J. Badger

STACKPOLE BOOKS

0 11557 02751 8

Copyright © 1998 by Stackpole Books

Published by
STACKPOLE BOOKS
5067 Ritter Road
Mechanicsburg, PA 17055

Printed in Hong Kong

10 9 8 7 6 5 4 3 2 1

First edition

All photographs by Curtis J. Badger unless otherwise credited.

Diagram and patterns by James D. Sprankle.

Library of Congress Cataloging-in-Publication Data

Badger, Curtis J.
     Carving and painting a green-winged teal with Jim Sprankle /
   Curtis J. Badger.
        p.   cm.
     ISBN 0-8117-2751-3
     1. Wood carving—Technique.   2. Painting—Technique.
3. Ducks in art.   I. Sprankle, James D.   II. Title.
TT199.7 .B333   1998
736'.4—dc21   97-29149
                                                       CIP

Contents

CHAPTER ONE

Jim Sprankle: From Baseball to Wild Birds

Jim Sprankle was one of major league baseball's original bonus babies. A hard-throwing right-hander, he was a natural, according to the scouts. As a teenager just graduated from high school in Lafayette, Indiana, he signed a contract with the Brooklyn Dodgers and took home $25,000. That was big money in 1952.

In those days a major-league baseball team might have fifteen or sixteen minor-league affiliates in cities and towns from coast to coast, border to border. Jim saw the country as a teenager dressed in Dodger blue, pitching his way across rural America, living every young man's dream. It was a life of golden promise, the dusty buses and one-night cheap hotels the price of admission to Ebbets Field, the land of the gods of Brooklyn, where toiled such immortals as Duke Snider, Carl Furillo, Jackie Robinson, Don Newcombe, and Pee Wee Reese.

Jim followed the grail for eleven years, chasing his future from Seattle to Cedar Rapids to Binghamton, until at age twenty-nine, he left the dream to the more innocent vision of younger men.

"When I stopped playing baseball, I went to work for a bank in Binghamton doing public relations and business development," says Jim. "And then I owned a refrigeration and restaurant supply business for six years. But I had always been interested in birds—I had been a taxidermist since I was sixteen—and I became involved in woodcarving in the 1960s while I was in business in New York. I used to come down to Tangier Island to go hunting, and I started learning about Chesapeake decoy makers such as Steve and Lem Ward. Then I found out about the Ward Foundation's World Championship Carving Competition, which really piqued my interest."

In the past twenty years, Jim has become one of America's leading wildfowl sculptors, winning more than seventy blue ribbons in national competitions and teaching in seminars throughout the country. He and his wife, Patty, run a successful mail-order carving supply business, his two books on wildfowl carving are selling well, and there is a waiting list for the summer workshops he holds around the country.

Jim Sprankle grew up in Indiana, on the Wabash and Tippecanoe Rivers. His grandfather, a German immigrant, was a talented cabinetmaker, and Jim learned from him a respect for wood and woodworking tools. An interest in ornithology led to a high school career in taxidermy, which provided a valuable background in avian anatomy and bone structure. These interests would later be focused in the art of sculpting waterfowl from wood.

"Anything that would fly fascinated me when I was growing up," he says. "At an early age ducks caught my fancy. An older kid who was a friend of mine went to Purdue University and studied waterfowl biology, and he would bring me ducks to mount every weekend. I just couldn't wait for him to get home so I could see what he had brought me. I'd stay up half the night mounting ducks. I think taxidermy triggered this desire to carve. It started with gunning decoys, because I wanted to make something that was better than the store-bought ones, and then it progressed to something more expressive."

Jim's career as an artist centered around waterfowl until a 1995 move to Sanibel Island, Florida. Frequent trips to such places as the J. N. "Ding" Darling National Wildlife Refuge on Sanibel encouraged him to take a fresh look at wading birds such as herons, egrets, and ibises. "I learned to carve after duck hunting in the Chesapeake Bay, and I lived in Annapolis and on the Eastern Shore for about twelve years, so waterfowl were part of my environment, and I specialized in ducks, especially teal. But when we moved to Florida, I was taken by the mangrove islands and the birds that inhabit them—tricolored herons, white ibises, roseate spoonbills—so I've done a number of pieces depicting these birds, which now are a part of my environment as well."

Jim began carving teal twenty-seven years ago because at that time it was easy to get small pieces of basswood, and he enjoyed being able to visualize and complete a carving project in a short period of time. "Teal appeal to me anyway," says Jim. "In my first competition I took three drakes, one of each species." I've probably carved more green-winged teal than any other bird." Teal—green-winged, blue-winged, and cinnamon—are our smallest ducks, making good subjects for beginning carvers because they are easy to handle and there is less surface texture to deal with than on a larger, more time-consuming bird.

Jim will carve the green-winged teal in this demonstration out of tupelo gum supplied by Curt's Waterfowl Corner in

Montegut, Louisiana. "Good tupelo is available, and I've found that it's easier for my workshop students to deal with. Tupelo is easy to carve and it doesn't have the fuzzing problems of basswood. It's also easy to sand, and it textures beautifully."

Jim will carve the teal with a variety of power tools. He will cut out the blank with a band saw, rough out the shape with a grinder, and then add fine detail with a high-speed grinder and a burning pen. The bird will be painted with Jo Sonja acrylics.

Jim at work on a piece depicting two scarlet ibises and a white ibis. He approaches each new project by learning as much as he can about his subject through extensive study and research.

Jim uses a study skin of a scarlet ibis to help prepare for painting the birds. He also uses reference photos and videotapes of live birds, as well as visits to zoos and aviaries, to achieve accuracy in color and detail in his painting.

Jim and Patty Sprankle, and Wiggles, at their Sanibel Island home.

Jim's time away from the studio is usually spent in his boat, fishing and bird-watching on the Gulf of Mexico or among south Florida's mangrove islands.

Jim at work on the teal drake in his studio.

DEAR WATERFOWL ARTIST:

Since 1984 I have been teaching waterfowl carving and painting seminars, first at my studio in Chester, Maryland, and now on Sanibel Island, Florida. Our fully air conditioned teaching facility is situated at Tarpon Bay, a spectacular lagoon which is part of the world famous J. N. "Ding" Darling Wildlife Refuge.

My carving sessions explore the use of research and reference materials, laying out patterns and roughing out the bird, laying out feather groupings, texturing and stoning, positioning of eyes and final preparation of birds for painting. My painting sessions will focus on use of acrylic paints, demonstration of blending and feather flicking, application of iridescents, use of the air brush, and sequences in painting the bird. A basic wood cutout of the subject bird will be supplied for the carving class, and one of my molded study birds will be provided for the painting class.

Our classes generally start at 1 p.m. on Sunday and continue through 6 p.m. Friday. The scope of the project will determine the duration of the class. We serve you a buffet lunch each day, as well as coffee and tea. For those of you needing accommodations, we can find you a place to stay for as little as $45 per night. The closest airport to Sanibel is Regional Southwest Airport in Ft. Myers, and Sanibel is about 35 minutes from the airport.

For those waterfowl artists who cannot make the trip to Florida, I also give many classes around the United States, as far west as California, Washington and North Dakota, Colorado, and of course Maryland and some of the more southern states. Rather than concentrating exclusively on ducks, I am teaching the carving and painting of wading birds as well, and have had an excellent response to our Scarlet Ibis, Blue Heron and Snowy Egret classes.

Our class size is limited to twelve, and because the size is small, we are able to offer personal teaching assistance to all levels of expertise, from the novice to the more accomplished artist looking for some "fine tuning". For more information on my classes here on Sanibel and at other locations, please write or call us at your convenience. If you prefer to use e-mail, our new address is Sprankle @ Cyberstreet. I will be happy to answer any questions you may have.

Sincerely,

Jim Sprankle

Greenwing Enterprises • 1147 Golden Olive Court • Sanibel Island, Florida 33957 • (941) 472-8666
Fax (941) 472-8445 • e-mail: sprankle@cyberstreet.com • web page: www.sprankle.com

CHAPTER TWO

About the Green-winged Teal

The green-winged teal drake, with its luminous green cheek patch and speculum, is one of our most colorful and popular waterfowl. The teal is known among artists for its beauty and among waterfowl hunters for its speed and ability to maneuver quickly in flight. Russ Williams, writing in *The Ways of Water-fowl,* claims that if there were a beauty pageant for ducks, "the dapper little green-winged teal would be a top-ranking contender . . . and if there were duck races he would probably be an easy winner." It is also our smallest North American waterfowl, and when spotted with flocks of black ducks or mallards, its diminutive size quickly becomes apparent.

The green-winged teal drake, which Jim Sprankle will be carving and painting in this demonstration, is easily identifiable, even at a distance. Its distinguishing characteristics are its reddish brown head, bright green elliptical cheek patch, green speculum, vertical white bar in front of the wings, and speckled breast. It is a remarkable combination of color and design, a great wildfowl art subject.

The teal is found throughout most of North America. It is one of the earliest spring migrants to head for northern breeding grounds in Canada, Alaska, and the northern continental United States. These hardy birds remain in the north until snow and freezing weather drive them southward to look for food. In mild winters, the birds will remain in the northern parts of their range.

Teal are dabbling ducks that feed in shallow streams, marshes, and sloughs, where they pluck weeds and grasses and forage for food in the muddy bottom. The majority of their diet is made up of vegetative material. Teal will leave the water to feed on acorns, berries, and seeds on land and will forage for waste grain in farm fields.

Teal usually nest away from the water, in hollows in the ground lined with soft grasses, leaves, and down. Nests are often hidden in clumps of grass, shrubs, or thickets. Seven to fifteen eggs are laid between May and August, and the female incubates them for twenty-one to twenty-three days. The young first fly at an estimated forty-four days, according to John K. Terres's *Audubon Society Encyclopedia of North American Birds*.

A flock of green-winged teal sounds from a distance like a chorus of spring peepers. If you find a group of them lounging on a shallow creek or in a freshwater swamp, you usually hear them before seeing them. If you're careful and quiet, you can sneak down to the shoreline to get a look at them without causing undue alarm. In late winter, teal will often congregate in protected areas that offer suitable habitat and food sources before heading north to the breeding grounds in early spring. Sometimes they gather in flocks of several hundred, often with black ducks, mallards, wigeon, gadwalls, and other dabbling ducks. To find such a flock is a real treat, especially if you have your binoculars with you and can spend some time studying the birds in detail, examining not only what they look like but how they act.

The most obvious thing is that teal are very small ducks, especially when seen with other dabblers. Another attribute that will become apparent is the speed and agility with which they fly. A flock of teal appears at first glance to be a flock of shorebirds that are flying in unison, turning and whirling as one, finally coming to rest in some shallow pocket of a salt-marsh pool.

If you can get a close look at a drake green-wing, perhaps with the low sun highlighting its green head patch and speculum, you'll understand why the teal has long been one of the favorite subjects of wildfowl artists in North America. Indeed, that experience would be a good introduction for this project. And if, during the course of carving and painting the teal, you should need a little inspiration, return to the place where the teal hang out. A few hours spent watching the birds can greatly motivate you to want to capture the beauty of this fascinating little bird.

This angle shows the tertial and scapular feather groups and will be good reference when carving these feathers (see chapter 9). Study this area also when painting the teal and note the light edges of the wings and the dark centers of the feathers across the back.

Vermiculation is the term used for the irregular lines that cover the sides of the teal. This photo will be a good guide when painting that area. Note that the vermiculated lines become lighter and less distinct along the belly of the bird; where the sides meet the breast, the lines become irregular dots.

This angle shows the confluence of the vermiculated lines of the sides and the irregular dots of the breast. Study the area where these two meet to get an idea of the shape of the lines and dots. Note also the white line separating the side pockets and breast and the white under-tail coverts.

The head of this teal is tucked into its body and turned slightly, just like the bird in this carving project. Notice the flow of the feathers along the head and compare these flow lines with the diagram in chapter 3. This angle also provides good color reference for use when painting the head. Note especially the light area under the eye and the subtle edges of the individual feathers.

TOM VEZO

TOM VEZO

The breast of the teal is champagne colored and covered with random dots, some darker and more distinct than others. On the carved bird, they are painted with a mix of carbon black and burnt umber and can be applied with either an airbrush or sable brush. Consult this photo for reference when painting the breast area.

TOM VEZO

CHAPTER THREE

Roughing Out

Jim begins the carving by tracing the top, side, and head patterns onto blocks of tupelo, and then cutting them out on a band saw. The tupelo block for the body is 10 by 5 by $3^{1/2}$ inches, slightly larger than the finished dimensions of the teal. He traces the side view pattern, and then the top view. The patterns provided in this chapter are to scale. To transfer a pattern to a block of wood, make a photocopy, cut around the outline, and then trace it onto the wood.

Jim emphasizes that the block should be square and the table of the band saw should be at a 90-degree angle to the blade. This will ensure that the dimensions of the bird will be the same on both sides and that the surfaces will be parallel. You can check the squareness of your block with a carpenter's square. If it's not square, you can square it on a jointer or take the block to a cabinet shop and have the work done there.

If you don't have a band saw, you can have a woodworking shop cut out the pattern for you. If you cut it yourself, be sure to understand and abide by the safety instructions supplied with your equipment. Power tools are extremely useful, but they can be dangerous if used improperly. If you are not experienced with them, have a professional woodworking shop do the cutting for you.

Jim cuts the side view first, then reattaches the top piece to cut out the top view. He uses small brads to fasten the two pieces together temporarily, inserting the brads in corners that will later be removed when the body of the bird is rounded off.

Jim saves the cut away pieces of the top and side views for later use. Excess wood is removed on the band saw, and the cutout is labeled with the date and project name and is saved for future use as a pattern.

The body and head patterns are cut out on the band saw, and Jim uses grinding tools to begin the preliminary shaping. He uses as reference a molded study bird he manufactures for use in carving and painting demonstrations (available from

Greenwing Enterprises, 1147 Golden Olive Court, Sanibel Island, FL 33957). If you don't have a study bird, a skin or taxidermy mount will do. The feather diagrams and layouts included in this chapter also will serve as guides for most of the fundamental measurements. A good general idea of the dimensions and anatomy can also be obtained by studying photographs and videotapes of teal and, of course, live birds, which can readily be found at most zoos and aviaries.

"You need to learn the anatomy of the bird," says Jim. "The head is turned slightly on the bird in our project, so the flank on the opposite side will be a little wider. You need to know how altering one aspect of the bird will affect another. You also need to know about the feather layout—where the major groups of flight feathers are located, and how they appear when the bird is in a certain position. It's time well spent to go to zoos and aviaries, and to study books and photographs dealing with bird anatomy."

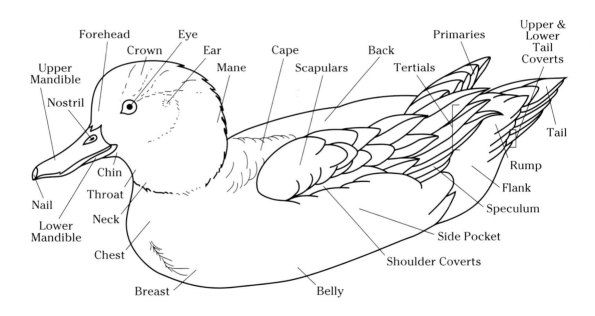

It's important to emphasize at this stage of the carving process the need for proper planning. Jim frequently sketches details onto the wood, planning how the rump will be shaped, where the tail feathers will lie, how the side pockets will be shaped. If you make an error in pencil, all you have to do is erase it. But if you make an error in carving, you likely will have to start over. So study the anatomy of the bird, be sure of your measurements, and use the pencil to create a blueprint for how the finished teal will look.

Another important consideration at this early stage, when much wood will be removed in a short time, is a way to remove dust particles from your work area. Jim uses a vacuum dust-removal system and a mask to avoid breathing dust. When carving with high-speed grinding tools, such a system is a must. Airborne dust particles are very hazardous to the respiratory system, and various dust-removal systems are on the market. In addition to his vacuum system and mask, Jim also has installed in his shop a commercial ceiling-mount air-filtering system.

In this chapter, Jim traces the patterns, cuts them out on the band saw, and then begins rounding out the carving with grinders, first a Makita, and then a Foredom with a rasplike cutter installed.

"This process is more like sculpting than carving," says Jim. "You're dealing with overall design and shape rather than details at this stage."

FEATHER LAYOUT

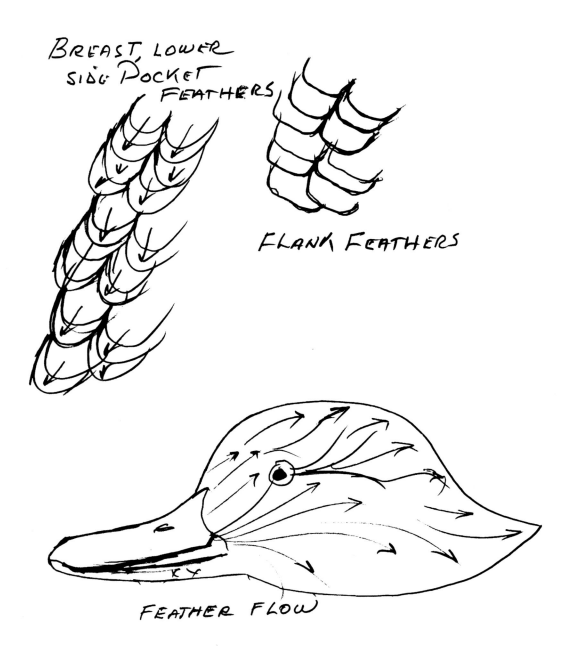

BREAST, LOWER SIDE POCKET FEATHERS

FLANK FEATHERS

FEATHER FLOW

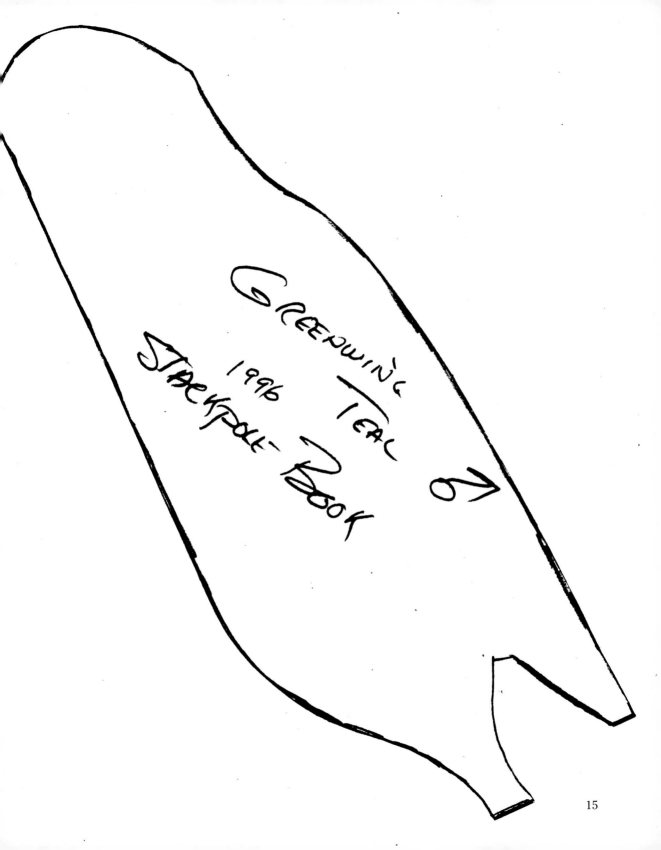

Greenwing Teal 6

1996

Stackpole Book

15

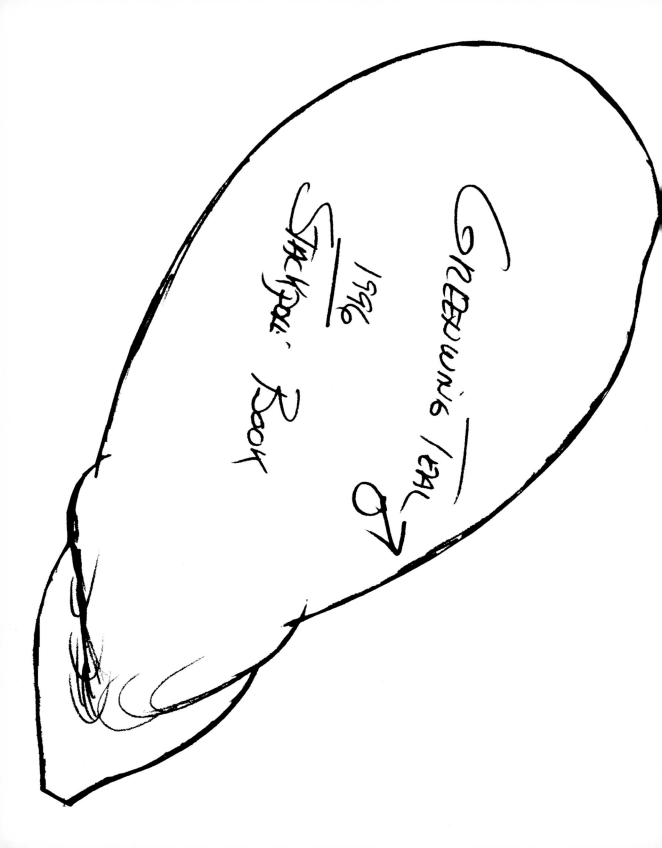

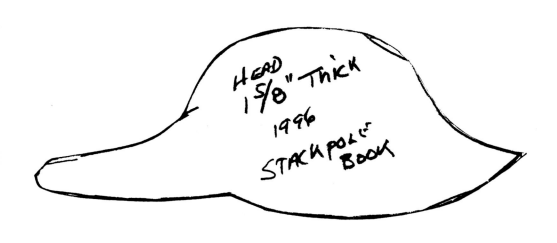

HEAD
1 5/8" THICK
1996
STACKPOLE BOOK

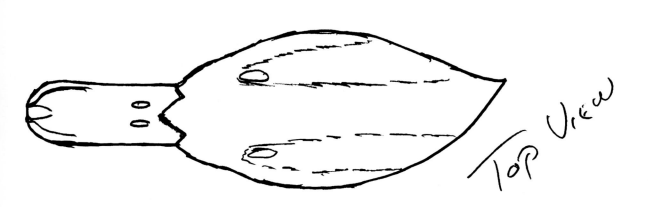

TOP VIEW

17

GREENWING TEAL ♂

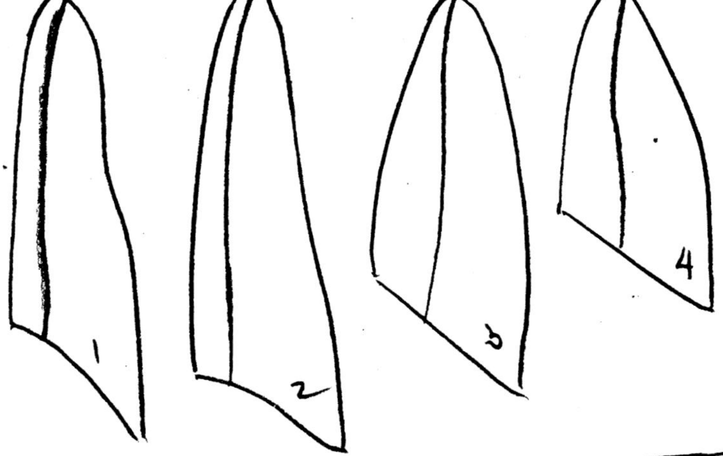

DISTANCE
EYE TO BILL
9MM MED BROWN

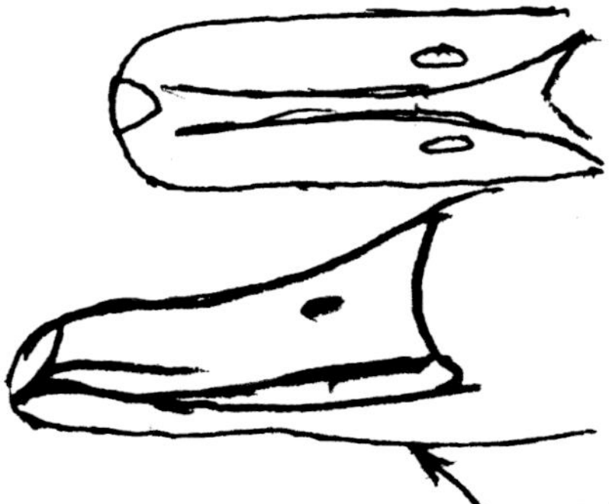

EXCESS
WOOD

OUTSIDE → TAIL FEATHER

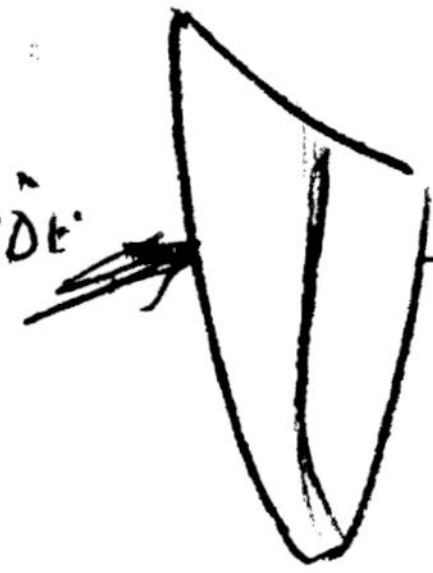

TERTIAL FEATHER

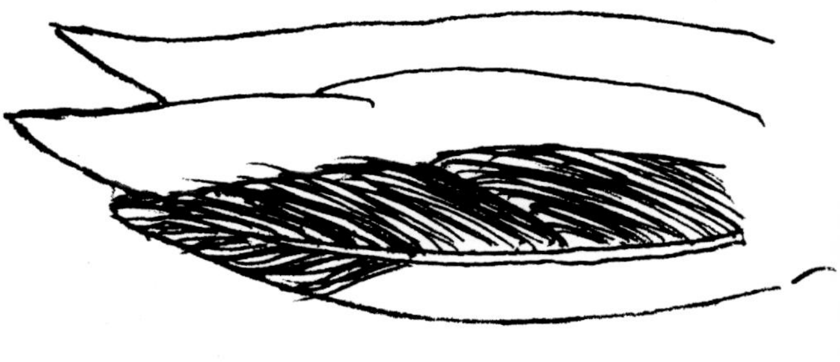

18

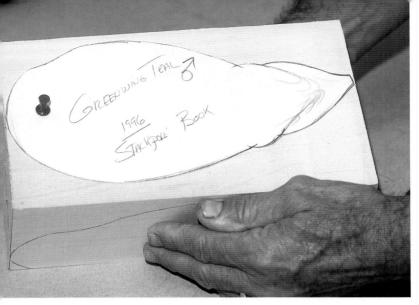

Jim begins by tracing a pattern onto a piece of tupelo whose sides have been squared. The blank is 10 by 5 by 3½ inches, slightly larger than the finished dimensions of the teal. The patterns included in this chapter are to scale. To transfer a pattern to a block of wood, make a photocopy, cut around the outline, and then trace it onto the wood.

The head pattern is sketched onto a piece of tupelo 1⅝ inch thick. Again, use the pattern included in this chapter, making a photocopy to avoid removing pages from the book.

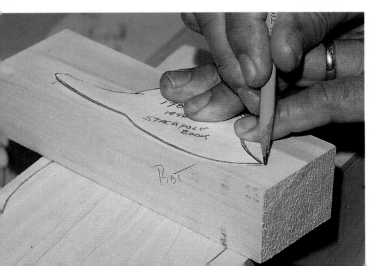

The head is positioned on the tupelo so that the length of the bill goes in the same direction as the grain of the wood. This provides added strength in what will be a fragile area of the carving.

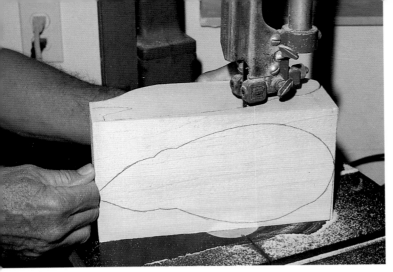

The teal is roughed out on a band saw. Jim emphasizes that the block of tupelo should be square, and the table of the band saw should be at a 90-degree angle to the blade. This will ensure that the dimensions of the bird will be the same on both sides and that the surfaces will be parallel.

Jim draws both the top and side patterns and cuts the side pattern first. When tracing the patterns, make sure the head is facing the same direction on both the top and sides. Use a square to ensure that the patterns are in alignment.

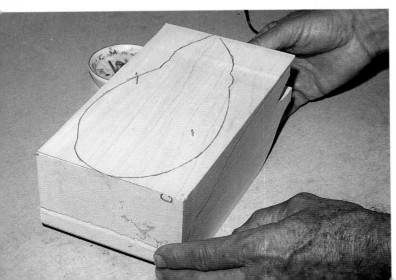

With the side profile cut, Jim reattaches the piece that has the top view profile. He uses small brads to fasten the two pieces together temporarily, inserting them in corners that will later be removed when the body is rounded off. Hot-melt glue could also be used for this step.

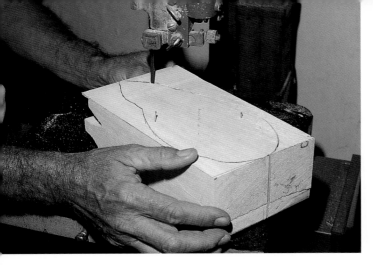

The top profile is carefully cut out on the band saw, following the lines traced from the paper pattern.

The head profile is roughed out on the band saw.

Jim saves the cut away pieces of the top and side views for later use. Excess wood is removed on the band saw, and the cutout is labeled with the date and project name and is saved for use as a pattern.

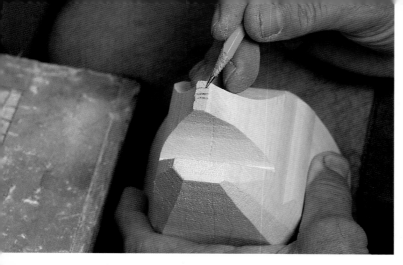

With the body and head profiles cut out, Jim is ready to begin the preliminary shaping of the bird. But first he sketches important details such as the various feather groups and dimensions such as the thickness of the tail. Here he has measured to find a center point, and then drawn another mark $1/8$ inch above and below that mark. The result will be a tail that is centered and $1/4$ inch thick.

That measurement is extended to the flank of the bird by first drawing a line perpendicular to the tail.

Jim then uses a 6-inch flexible ruler to extend the markings he made on the tip of the tail to the perpendicular line.

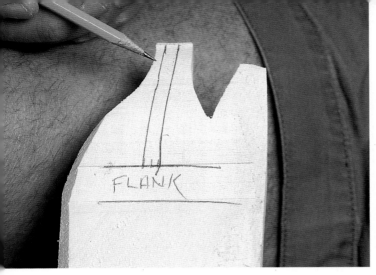

A center mark is made on the perpendicular line, and then two others 1/8 above and below the center. The marks are then connected, thus laying out the side of the tail. The same procedure is repeated on the other side.

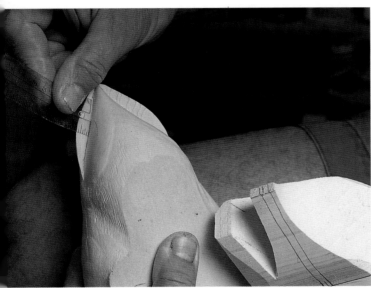

Jim uses one of his molded study birds, *left,* as reference, transferring measurements from the molded bird to the wooden one with the plastic ruler or dividers. If you don't have a study bird, a study skin or taxidermy mount will do. The feather diagrams and layouts included in this chapter also give guidance for most of the fundamental measurements.

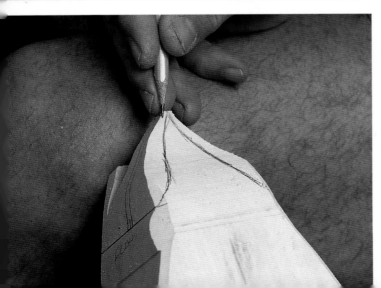

The head and tail of this teal are turned slightly, so it's important to sketch various areas of the bird now, before removing wood. Here Jim sketches the position of the rump. "It's important to study anatomy, to realize that turning the head will also slightly extend the flank area on the opposite side from which it's turned," says Jim.

23

The tail is now roughed in with pencil. The thickness is measured and laid out, and the rump, the area under the tail, is sketched. The areas marked with Xs indicate wood that will be removed.

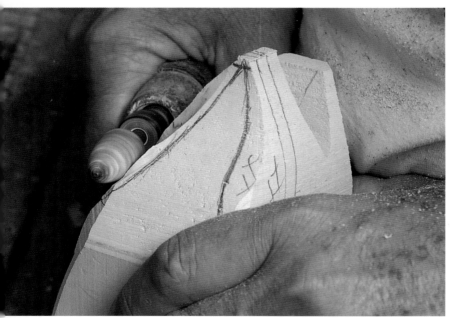

The next stage of roughing out begins under the tail, and Jim uses a Makita grinder, which removes a great deal of wood in a short time and is excellent for roughing-out procedures such as this.

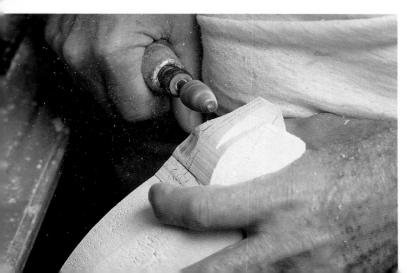

Jim uses the grinder to cut right up to the pencil lines, removing the wood that had been Xed out in the preliminary sketching process.

Jim uses a dust-removal system and a mask to avoid breathing dust. When carving with high-speed grinding tools, such a system is a must. Airborne dust particles are hazardous to the respiratory system, and there are various dust-removal systems on the market. Jim uses a vacuum system that pulls dust particles away from his work area through the wire grate *(left)*. He also wears a mask and has installed a commercially made ceiling-mount air-filtering system.

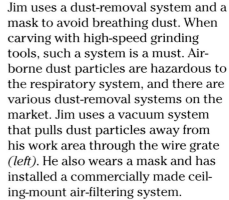

The Makita grinder at rest. The interchangeable cutting tips can be used for a wide variety of roughing-out procedures.

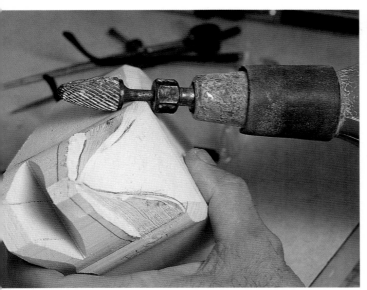

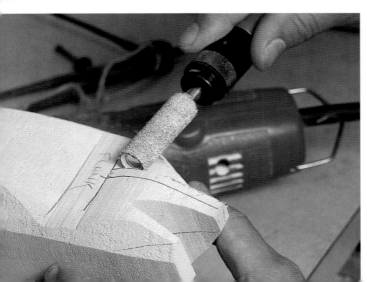

After using the grinder, Jim moves to a somewhat less aggressive tool, a carbide cutter on a Foredom flexible-shaft grinder. The cutter is 2 inches long and 1/2 inch in diameter. The texture is similar to that of a rasp.

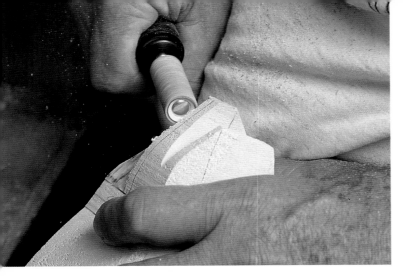

The Foredom with the carbide cutter is used to refine the shape of the rump and tail feathers.

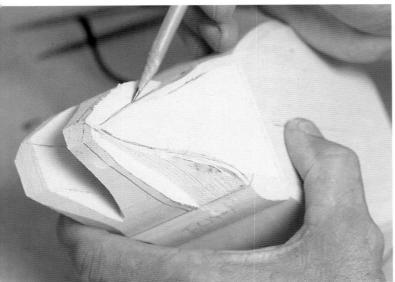

The rump area is now roughed out, reduced to the proper dimensions, and ready for more detailed carving.

Before going further, Jim uses the pencil to reestablish important details that have been obscured in carving, such as the angle of the rump.

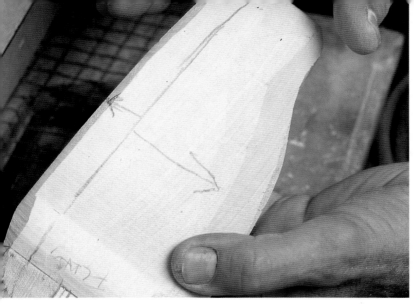

With the rump roughed out, Jim will now round out the body. He draws a horizontal line approximately one-third of the way up the sides to guide him in removing wood along the flanks. Everything above that line will be rounded toward the back, and the body beneath the line will be rounded toward the bottom of the bird.

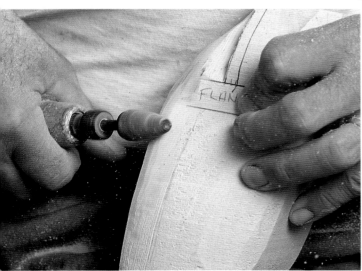

Jim begins below the horizontal line, using the Makita grinder to round off the body. The curvature should be gentle; think of the lines as forming an imaginary circle above and below the body of the bird, Jim advises.

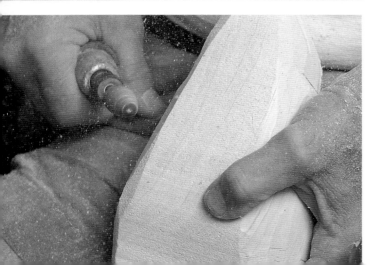

The grinder is used to round off the top of the body. This part of the carving process is more like sculpting than carving; you are dealing with overall design and shape rather than details at this stage.

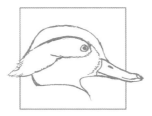

CHAPTER FOUR

Adding Details

With the carving roughed out, Jim is ready to begin adding details and reducing parts of the bird to their proper dimensions. For example, he will lay out and carve the side pockets of the teal, the areas that lie below the folded wings and between the rump and breast. To do this, he will sketch the outline of the area in pencil, then cut a groove along the line with the carbide cutter in the Foredom tool. The edge of the groove will then be softened with the same tool.

Jim will also lay out the neck and breast area and begin reducing these parts of the teal to their proper dimensions.

As in the previous chapter, an understanding of waterfowl anatomy is important here, as is reference material such as taxidermy mounts, study skins, photographs, or, Jim's preference, a molded cast made of an earlier wood carving. Jim uses these casts in his carving and painting seminars, and he uses a teal cast in this chapter to transfer dimensions to the carving.

With the carving roughed out, the first step is to lay out and carve the side pockets, the areas that lie just below the wings. Jim uses dividers to transfer the dimensions of the side pockets from his cast study bird to the woodcarving.

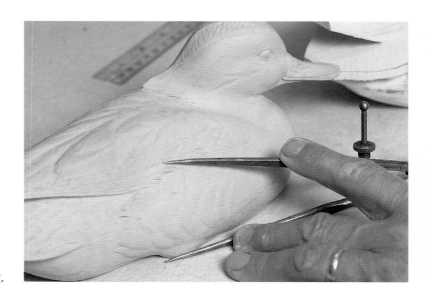

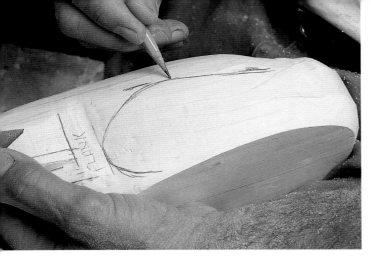

The side pockets run from the flanks to the breast of the bird. Jim sketches the outline of the area with a pencil.

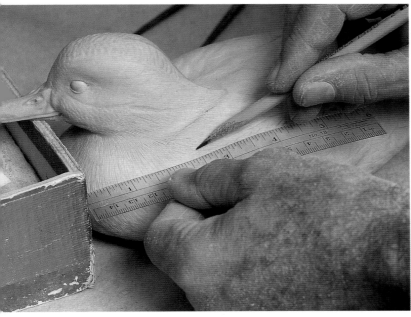

Measurements are checked against the study bird with the 6-inch plastic ruler.

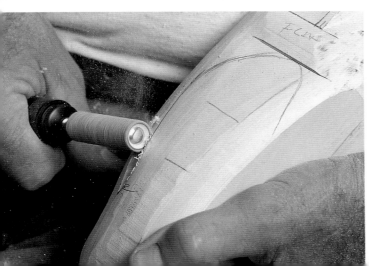

Jim takes off a small amount of wood at a time as he cuts along the pencil line, working first on one side and then the other, frequently checking his measurements.

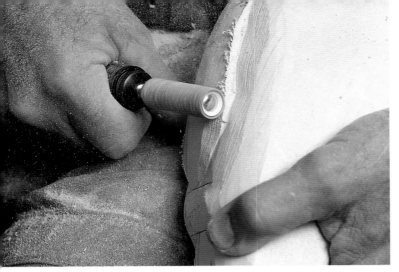

Jim defines the side pockets by carving a ledge along the pencil line and then softening the edge and creating a gentle slope.

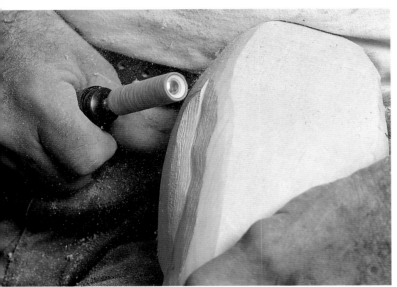

The 2-inch carbide cutter is used to cut the groove and to bevel the edge, as shown here. Keep this edge subtle, Jim advises, or the side pockets will look like saddlebags.

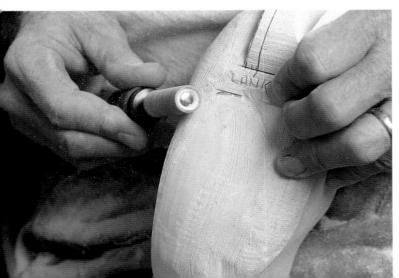

The tops of the side pockets have been shaped, and here Jim uses the carbide cutter to create a gradual curve where the side pockets meet the bottom of the carving.

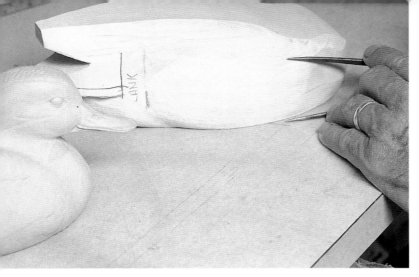

Jim removes a small amount of wood, then checks his progress by comparing the measurements of the carving with those of the study bird. He does this numerous times during the carving process.

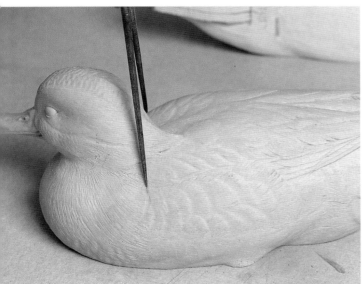

With the side pockets shaped, Jim lays out the area where the shoulders and the crest meet. On the study bird, he measures from the top of the side pockets on each side to find the width of the back.

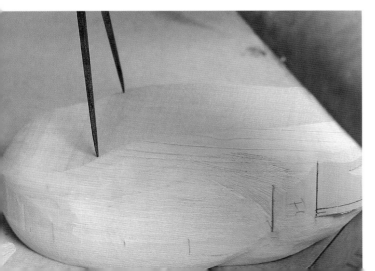

This measurement is transferred to the carving. Then, by halving the width, Jim establishes the center of the back.

Before doing further carving, Jim uses the pencil to reestablish the side pocket dimensions on both sides. It's important, he says, to maintain benchmarks such as these throughout the carving process.

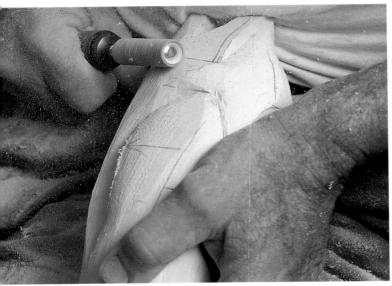

Jim rounds off the top of the bird, above the side pockets. Note the horizontal line one-third of the way up from the bottom. It's the same line Jim established earlier, helping him to "carve to the round."

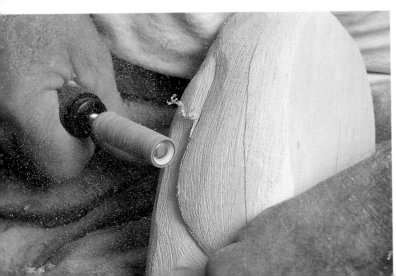

Jim now carves the shoulder area of the teal, reducing the width to the dimension he transferred from the study cast.

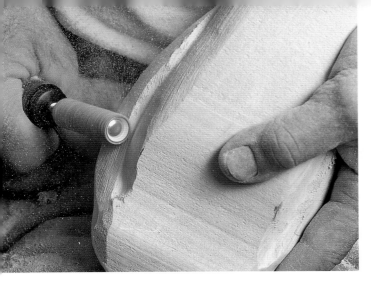

With the two pencil marks as a guide, Jim notes that the width at this point is now correct.

The final steps in this preliminary carving process are to round off the back and to define the wings and do some preliminary carving of them. Jim sketches these details with the pencil.

Two "safety lines" are drawn on the back to guide Jim as he rounds off the area. He will not round off the body above those lines; wood must be left there to carve the wings, which lie across the back.

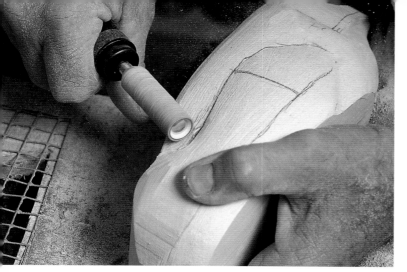

The 2-inch carbide cutter is used to round off the body above the side pockets.

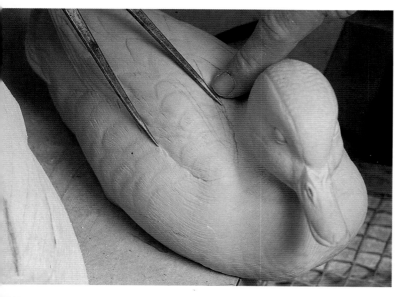

Jim will rough-shape the wings, using dimensions transferred from the study bird. He uses dividers to measure the width of the right wing and transfers this measurement to the wooden bird.

Jim sketches on the bird quite a bit while carving. The lines here show how the wings will fold over the body, with the cape, the separation between them, behind the head and crest.

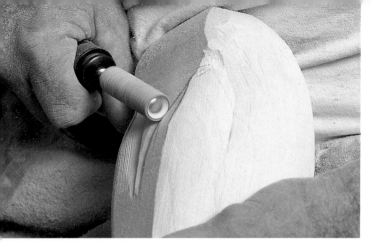

The separation between the wings is carved with the 2-inch carbide cutter, and this completes the preliminary sculpting of the bird. The next step is to carve the head, but first Jim will sand the body and remove the tool marks left by the carbide cutter.

Jim uses two power sanding tools. An 8-inch pneumatic drum is used for broader areas, such as the back and sides and broader contours.

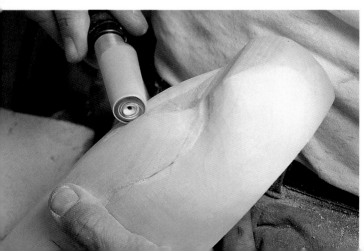

A split mandrel loaded with 150-grit paper is used on a Foredom tool to sand the harder-to-reach places. Later, Jim will use finer paper for finish sanding. "No matter what kinds of sanding tools you use, you'll always need to do some hand sanding," he says. He attaches the paper onto a thin rubber pad to make handling it easier.

CHAPTER FIVE

Carving the Head

The head was cut from tupelo $1^5/8$ inch thick, so the width is already correct. Jim's first step is to draw a centerline and then lay out and do the preliminary carving of the bill. He uses a paper template, which is reproduced on page 18.

The two major tasks in carving the head are the carving of the bill and the cutting of the two eye channels. Proper reference material is essential for both steps. You can use study casts, taxidermy specimens, photographs, or all of the above. These will serve as a road map or blueprint as you go about carving.

One of the keys in this chapter is symmetry. The bill must be centered, so establishing the centerline is important, as is proper use of the pattern. Symmetry is also important when cutting the eye channels: One must not be higher or lower than the other. As you're carving, check frequently to make sure the channels are at the same depth and angle, and use the "pencil test" described in this chapter.

Jim uses his Foredom tool with the 2-inch carbide cutter for most of the general shaping of the head. He uses a tapered stone to shape the cheeks and a split mandrel with 150-grit paper to sand the head and remove tool marks.

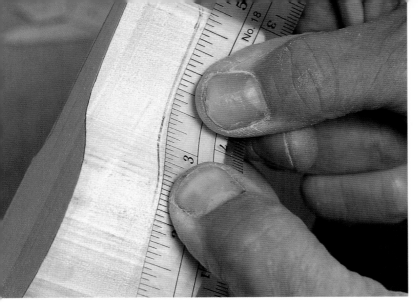

The first step in carving the head is to establish a centerline. Jim does this by halving the width, 1⁵⁄₈ inch, coming up with ¹³⁄₁₆. He uses the flexible ruler to draw the line.

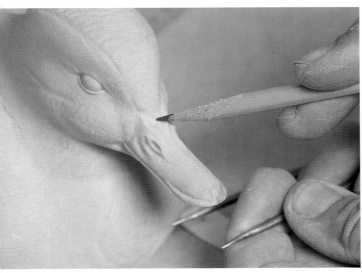

Again, the study bird is used as reference for measurement. Here Jim uses dividers to measure the length of the bill, beginning at the center at the culmen, the fleshy tissue where the bill joins the head.

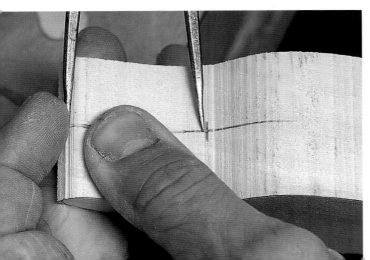

He transfers that measurement to the woodcarving and makes a mark that will represent the spot where the center of the bill meets the culmen.

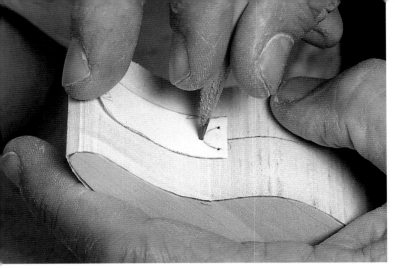

The area where the bill meets the head is not straight or flat, but somewhat triangular. A paper template (see page 18) is used to determine the corners of the triangle and the width and shape of the bill. The pencil is used to align the center of the template with the mark made earlier on the centerline.

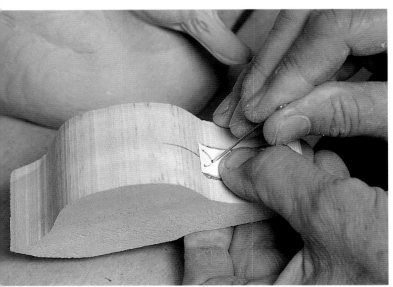

A pin is used to mark the locations of the corners of the bill, and these will later be used as benchmarks when measuring and laying out the upper and lower mandibles.

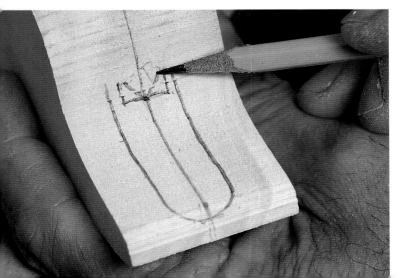

Jim refers to the center of the culmen as point B and the two outer corners as points A. The lower corners of the upper mandible will be points C, and tip of the bill is referred to as point D. By connecting point A and point B, the triangular shape of the culmen is set, and the dimensions are correct. These points will later be used to lay out and carve the separation between the mandibles, nostrils, nail, and other details in the bill area.

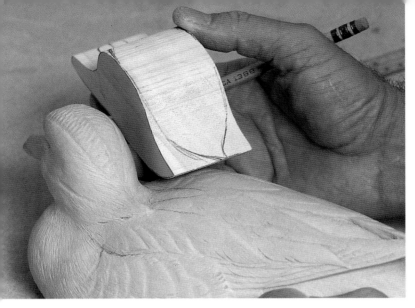

Before carving the bill, Jim lays out the crest of the teal, referring to the study bird for the shape. With the head turned slightly, the crest will not be symmetrical.

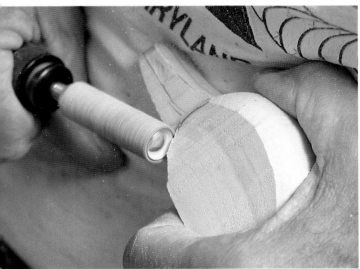

Carving begins with the 2-inch carbide cutter in the Foredom tool. Jim reduces the width of the bill, following the contour of the face.

Rough-shaping of the bill is complete, and it is reduced to what will be the final dimensions. It will be detailed in the next chapter.

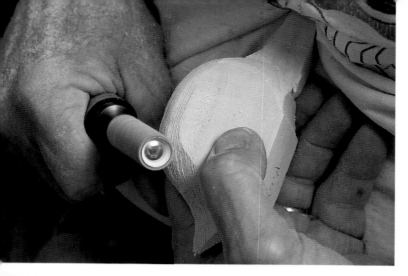

The top of the head and the crest are carved with the carbide cutter, following the sketch drawn earlier.

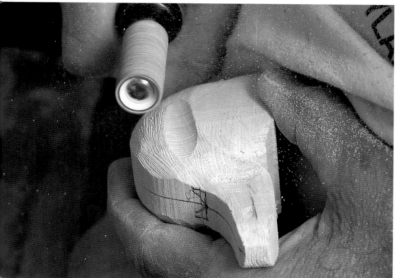

The carbide cutter is used to cut grooves along both sides of the head. These represent the eye channels.

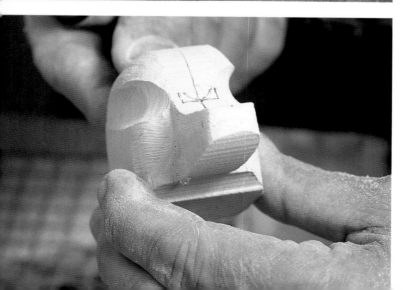

The channels should be in alignment and at the same depth.

A pencil line helps Jim check the eye channels for alignment. Although the eyes will not be inserted until later, now is the time to lay the foundation for them, making sure that the contours of the face are carved properly.

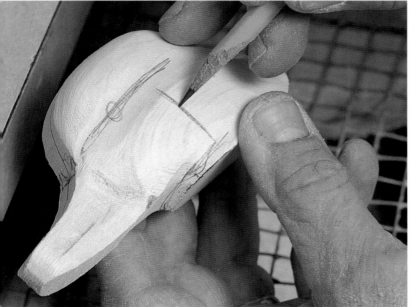

Jim sketches the eye in position, and he draws a vertical line through the center of the head. This line represents the high point of the facial contour. The head will be carved from that line toward the face and toward the back of the head, creating the proper contour.

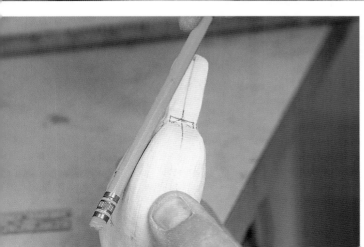

An easy way to ensure that the eye channel is angled properly is to give it the "pencil test." The angle should be toward the tip of the bill. If the angles from both eye channels intersect at the tip of the bill, you'll know the alignment and the angle are good.

Jim uses a tapered stone on his Foredom grinder to shape the cheeks of the teal, working away from the pencil line.

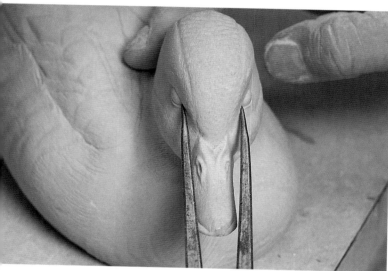

The width of the head at the eye position is checked with dividers on the cast bird.

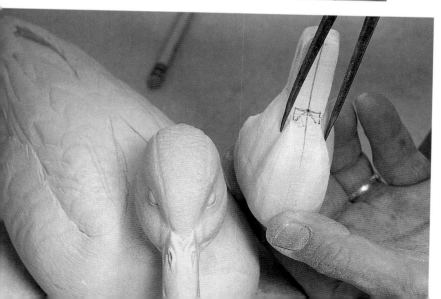

That measurement is then transferred to the carving, ensuring that the width is correct.

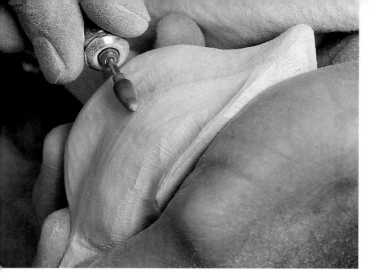

A small stone in the NSK high-speed grinder smooths the eye channel.

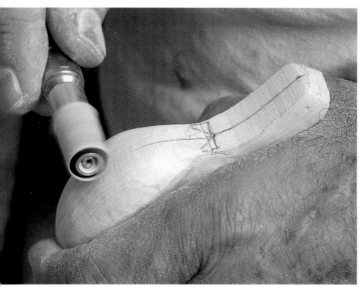

Prior to carving the upper and lower mandibles, Jim sands the bill and head. These areas will be easier to detail with the wood surface smooth and ready to sketch on and cut.

CHAPTER SIX

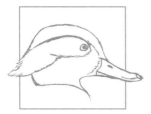

Carving the Bill

Jim established the general dimensions of the bill in the previous chapter with the paper template, and now he will add details. He again uses the cast bird as reference, transferring dimensions from it to the carving. Early on, he reestablishes his six reference points: at the center of the bill and the front edge of the culmen, at the corners of the culmen, at the tip of the bill, and at the top rear corners of the upper mandible. These guide him in laying out and carving the separation between the mandibles, the culmen, the nostrils, and the nail.

Jim does most of the carving of the bill with a small knife, but a grinder or burning pen could be used. He feels that the knife gives him more control in carving, although he does use the burning pen to clean some of the knife cuts and to add details such as the serration on the bottom edge of the upper mandible and the wrinkles on the lower mandible. He uses a grinder with a sharp dental bit to drill the nostrils. As always, good reference material is essential when carving such an intricate area. Study casts or close-up photographs are essential.

Jim redraws the centerline and reference points at the culmen. Then, with a sharp knife, he cuts from point A, the outer corner of the triangle, to point B, the center, on each side of the culmen, with the knife blade held perpendicular to the surface of the wood, leaving a small crown, or bump, to represent the culmen.

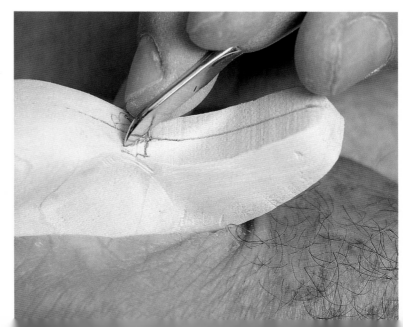

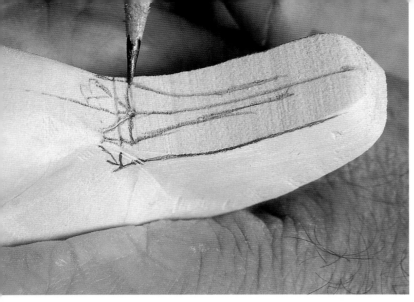

He then uses a pencil to sketch the top edge, or ridge, of the bill. It begins at the outer points of the culmen triangle, curves inward, and extends along the centerline.

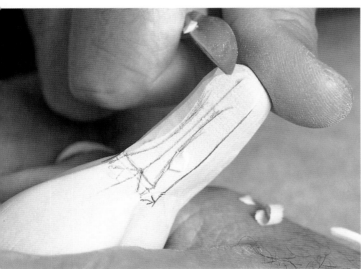

A carving knife is then used to remove wood on both sides of the bill, rounding and thinning it.

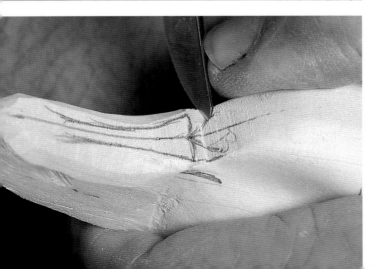

The bill is then carved back to where the cuts had earlier been made along the culmen.

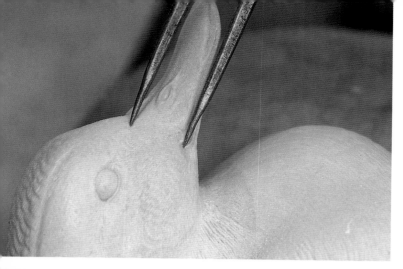

Now Jim is ready to determine the position of points C, the lower rear corners of the upper mandible. On the study bird, he uses the dividers to measure from the outer corner of the culmen (point A) to the corner of the upper mandible.

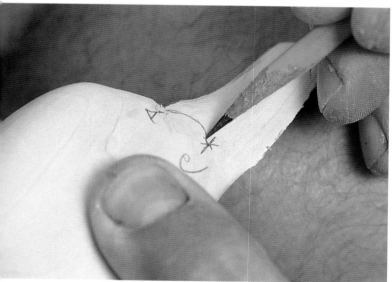

This measurement is transferred to the carving on each side and the points are marked C. A curved line representing the base of the bill is drawn on both sides, and Jim makes sure they are symmetrical before carving the area.

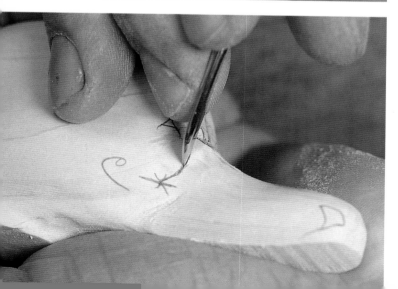

He uses a sharp carving knife to cut a line about 1/8 inch deep along that line, holding the blade at a 90-degree angle to the wood. He then carves the bill back to that line in the same way he carved the top of the bill.

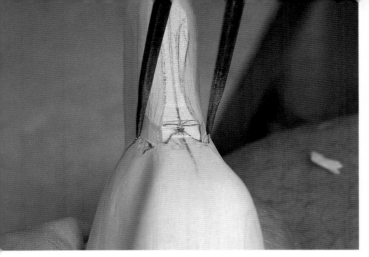

The base of the bill is now defined, and Jim checks the dimensions against the cast bird. Essentially, he cut a line perpendicular to the surface around the base of the bill, then removed wood from the bill, working back to that line.

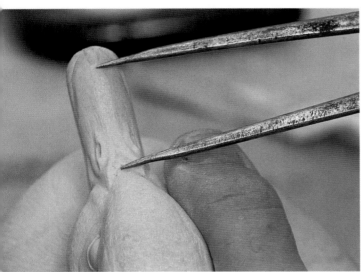

Now Jim will lay out and carve the nail, the raised area at the very tip of the bill. He again refers to the study bird, measuring with the dividers from the culmen to the nail.

That measurement is transferred to the carving, the nail is sketched in pencil, and then it is carved with the knife as shown. Jim carves the nail at this point because it makes the next step, defining the separation between the mandibles, much easier.

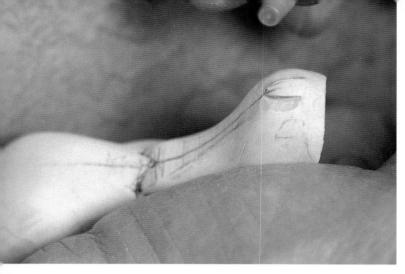

If you're more comfortable using high-speed grinders, you could do the job with one of them and a diamond burr cutter, as Jim demonstrates here.

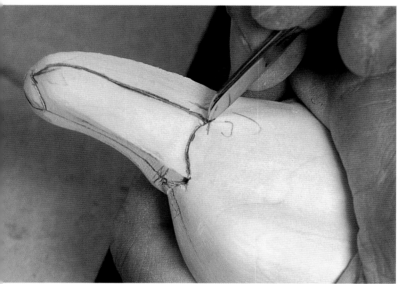

The bottom of the upper mandible is sketched in pencil, and then the knife is used to make a cut along that line, which begins on each side at point C and runs forward to point D, the bottom of the nail at the tip of the bill.

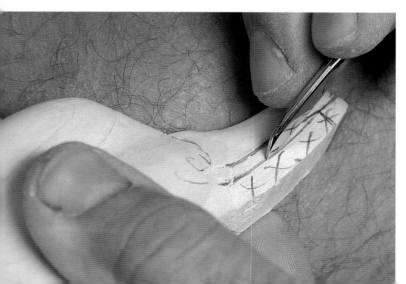

A second line, representing the bottom of the lower mandible, is also drawn and cut. Material below the lower mandible, indicated by the Xs, will be removed. Note that the lower mandible is visible near the head but tucks under the upper mandible about halfway along the length of the bill.

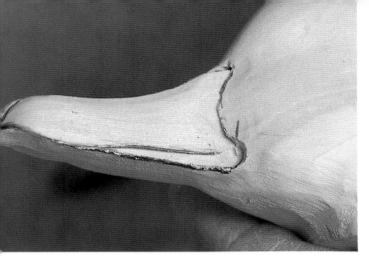

With the wood removed, the bill looks like this. At this point, the head and bill are carved to the proper shape. Now comes the more intricate task of adding details that will make the carving lifelike and realistic.

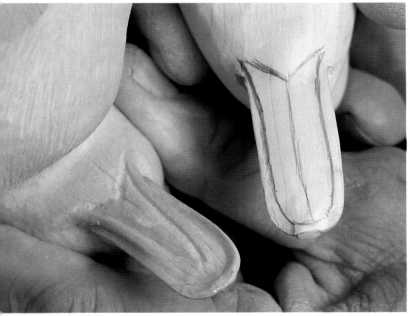

A look at the study bird shows how the lower mandible fits under the upper one. Jim sketches the outer edge of the lower mandible with the pencil and draws a centerline that will represent the bottom of the lower mandible.

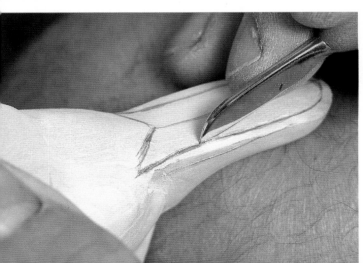

The separation between the mandibles is carved with the knife, first by pressing the blade at a 90-degree angle to the wood along the line just drawn.

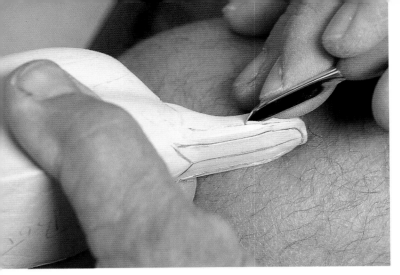

The same technique is used on the line on the upper mandible. Where these two knife cuts meet, the wood will be removed.

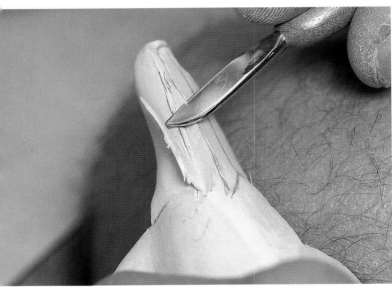

Jim carefully removes the wood with the knife blade. The lower mandible is not as wide as the upper one, and this step visually creates the lower mandible by separating it from the upper.

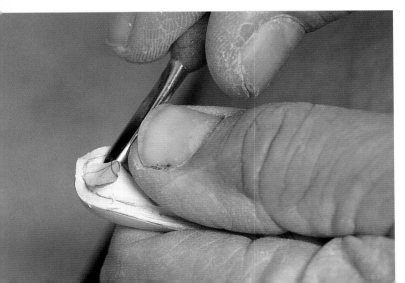

The knife is used to remove wood under the bill. At this point on the bill, the lower mandible is tucked inside the upper one, so this area is reduced, creating the impression of the upper mandible overlapping the lower one.

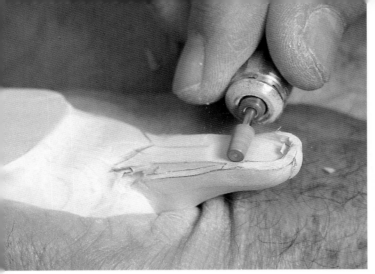

Jim uses the high-speed grinder with a diamond tip to further define this area. The separation between the mandibles is now apparent. "Check your reference material often when working in detailed areas like this," Jim advises. Molded casts, taxidermy specimens, live birds, and photographs are all useful.

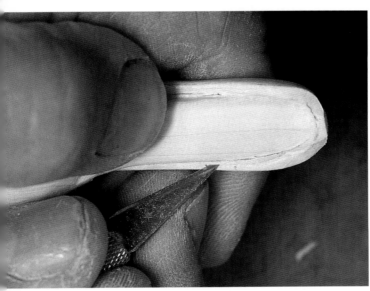

Jim uses a number 11 X-acto blade to undercut the edge of the upper mandible, separating it from the lower one.

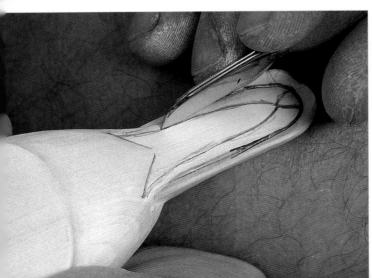

The bottom of the lower mandible is carved with the knife and a burning pen. Here Jim cuts along a pencil line that will yield a groove around the lower mandible. The cut is then cleaned with the burning pen.

The burning pen is also used to carve the serration on the membrane of the upper mandible and to create small wrinkles at the base of the lower one.

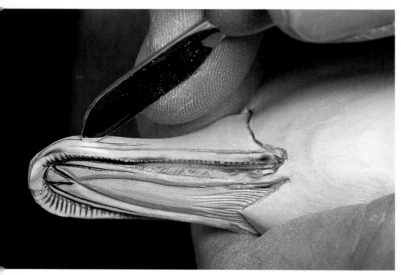

The knife is used to carve a small groove along the lower edge of the upper mandible, creating a lip. A diamond cutter or burning pen could be used, but Jim prefers the control he has with a knife.

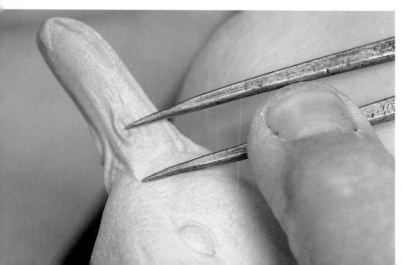

The next step is to lay out and carve the nostrils. Jim uses the dividers to measure the location on the study bird, then he transfers the measurement to the carving.

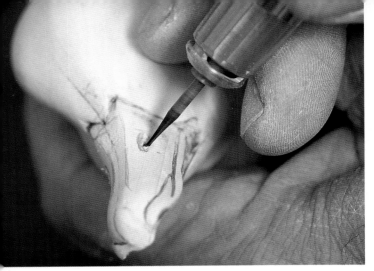

A small dental burr in the high-speed grinder is used to drill the nostril hole, which goes all the way through the bill. Jim carves from first one side, then the other, thus ensuring that the holes will be in alignment.

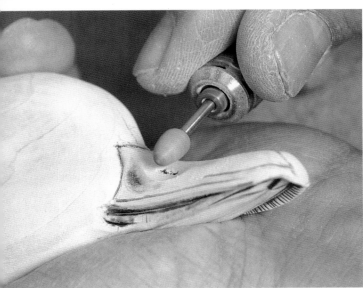

After drilling the holes, Jim uses a rounded diamond cutter to reduce the area around the nostrils, creating a slight depression. An epoxy membrane will be added here later.

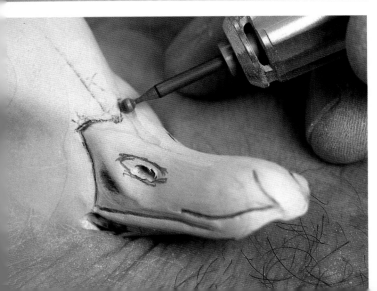

A small ball on the high-speed grinder is used to define the area where the bill meets the head.

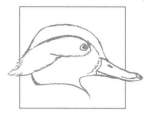

CHAPTER SEVEN

Inserting the Eyes

Jim uses the molded bird to determine the position of the eyes, measuring from the culmen to the center of the eye channel. "If you err, err on the side of placing the eyes too far forward," he advises. "The bird has a more alert, intelligent look that way." He sketches the eye position, then uses pushpins to help check alignment. The pins also indicate the angle at which the eye holes will be drilled, which is perpendicular to the surface of the eye channel.

The holes are drilled with a tapered cutter designed for this purpose. Jim drills one side first, establishes a good fit, and then drills the second hole, which is cut slightly larger than the first one, allowing for some degree of adjustment when the glass eye is inserted. The eyes must be in alignment, at the same depth, and in the same vertical plane. When viewed from the top of the head, only a small amount of each eye should be visible.

Jim uses 9mm glass eyes. He sets the eyes in Plastic Wood brand filler and uses lacquer thinner and a brush to feather the edges. "A common mistake when setting the eyes is using too much Plastic Wood," he says. "It's hard to remove it once you put it on. You also need to feather the edges very finely and not leave an edge. The eye is a very important part of the carving. It's where the viewer's attention is drawn, so you need to make sure the eye insertion is done right, with the proper alignment and depth."

Jim frequently adds a second, thin coat of Plastic Wood just to make sure the edges are feathered and are not abrupt. He also will use some of the compound to build up the brow area slightly, giving the drake a more masculine look.

The Plastic Wood takes about an hour to dry. Jim usually inserts the eyes just before taking a lunch break so that the material will be workable when he returns.

The eye location is determined by measuring from the culmen to the eye channel. A cast bird or taxidermy specimen could be used as reference, or you can use Jim's measurement according to the patterns on page 17.

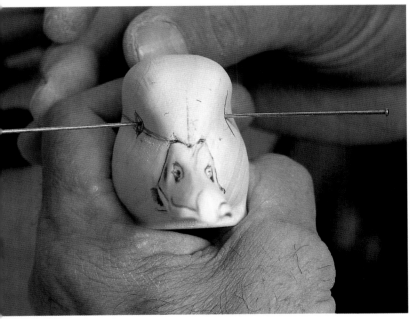

The pushpins are used to check alignment and to indicate the angle at which the eye holes will be drilled.

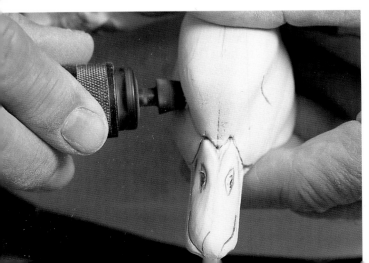

The holes are drilled with a tapered cone designed for this purpose. It is available from carving supply retailers, including Jim's Greenwing Enterprises (see p. 5 for address). Jim drills the right side first, testing the fit of the 9mm glass eye as he drills. When he establishes a good fit, he then drills the second hole.

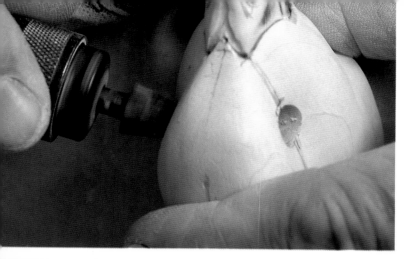

The second hole is cut slightly larger than the first one, allowing for some degree of adjustment when the glass eye is inserted. The eyes must be in alignment, at the same depth, and in the same vertical plane.

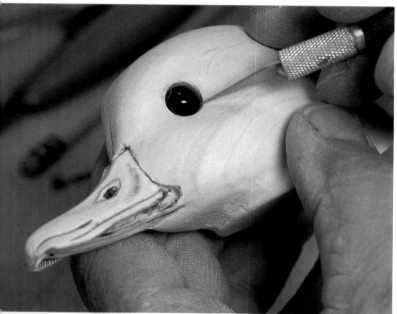

The left eye fits easily into the hole drilled for it. The eye will be embedded in Plastic Wood filler.

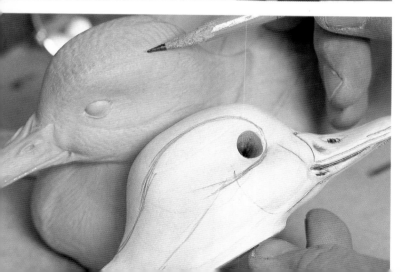

Before inserting the eye, Jim sketches the area along the head where the green cheek patch is located.

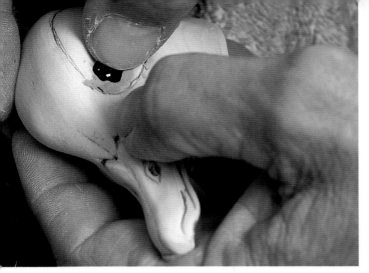

Plastic Wood is placed in the eye holes, and the glass eye is pressed into position.

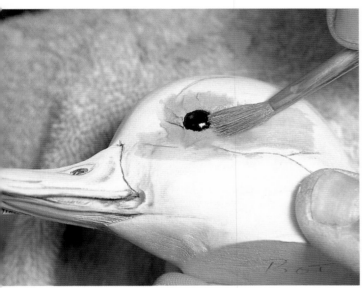

Lacquer thinner and a brush are used to feather the edges.

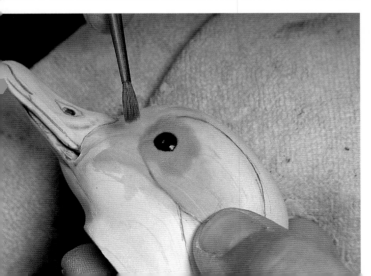

The lacquer thinner makes the putty easy to work with the brush or a finger. Jim uses a small amount to build up the brow area slightly.

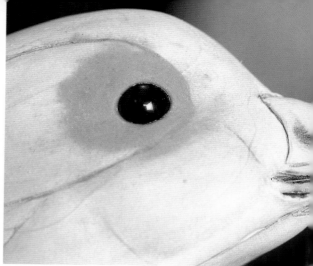

(top, left) Jim adds a second, thin coat of Plastic Wood to the eye to make sure the edges are feathered and are not abrupt. The edge of the Plastic Wood must not show when the bird is painted.

(top, right) The eye has been inserted, the edge of the putty feathered out, and in about an hour it will be dry enough to work on.

(left) While Jim has the Plastic Wood out, he uses some to create the small nub on the side of the body where the leg is located.

(bottom) Again, the area is shaped with a brush and lacquer thinner, and the edges are feathered so that they will not be obvious.

CHAPTER EIGHT

Texturing and Attaching the Head

Jim prefers to texture the head before attaching it to the body. "I have far better control of the head when I can hold it in my hands than when it is attached to the body of the bird," he says. He first uses a pencil to lay out the direction of the feather flow. The feathers are small near the base of the bill and increase in size as they near the eyes (see the pattern on page 14). It's important that the wood be thoroughly sanded and have a very smooth surface before sketching the feathers.

When sketching, or painting, Jim holds the pencil (or brush) against his body and moves the work object. "I like to have everything locked against my body," he says. "It gives me more control to have my hand stationary and braced as I sketch."

Once Jim has sketched the feathers, he uses a white round ball in his high-speed grinder to relieve them. "This tool polishes the wood instead of grinding it away," he says. "You could use a diamond tip, but I feel that the diamond removes too much wood. I use a ball, and it's important to keep in mind that the smaller the ball, the tighter the radius you can turn. So a small-diameter ball is especially good for relieving the small feathers on the front part of the head behind the bill. I use a larger ball on the larger feathers on the back of the head."

After relieving the feathers of the head, Jim smoothes the area with 400-grit sandpaper. Then he uses a pencil to reestablish the location of the feathers. It is important to visually maintain the distinct margins of the feathers, because individual barbs will later be added to each feather.

Jim begins at the crest and works forward as he relieves feathers. He uses the diamond inverted stone for the long, sweeping feathers of the crest. "These are more like hair than feathers, really, so I'm just making fine lines following the feather flow I established with the pencil," he says. "I use the diamond where the texture is coarse and will use the ball on the smaller, finer feathers farther forward on the head."

Jim also uses a tool called a "little saw," a thin disk with a sharp cutting edge. This is handy for carving the long, sweeping feathers at the very edge of the crest.

A burning pen could be used here, but Jim prefers various cutting tools. "When you're using white paint, it's difficult to get it soft and warm looking if you put it on over a surface that has been burned. With a stone, you get a wider line that's not as deep, and it gives you a softer look."

Jim uses texturing techniques as a foundation for painting. For example, he uses the burning pen to create a subtle depression, or dimple, between feathers. Since the feathers are somewhat lighter in color near the quill, these dimples will later be painted a shade lighter than the surrounding area. Techniques such as this add interest and realism to a carving. "If you haven't prepared for this detail by carving, it's very difficult to accomplish just by painting alone," says Jim. "So the time to plan your painting techniques is now, while you're adding texture. There is a strong correlation between carving and painting."

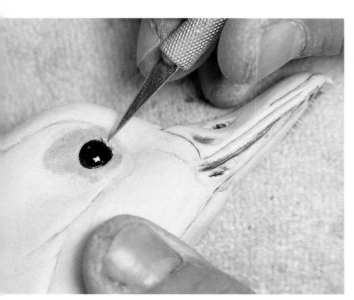

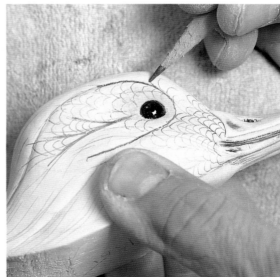

Before texturing the head, Jim uses an X-acto knife to clean putty from around the eye.

The first step is to lay out the feather flow—the direction in which the feathers lie. The feathers are small near the base of the bill and increase in size as they near the eyes (refer to the diagram on page 14).

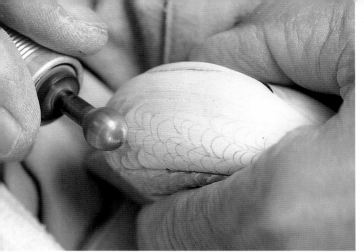

Once Jim has sketched the feathers, he uses a ball in his high-speed grinder to relieve the outline of each feather, following the pencil lines. "This tool polishes the wood instead of grinding it away," he says. This large ball is used on the top and back of the head, a smaller one on the small feathers at the base of the bill.

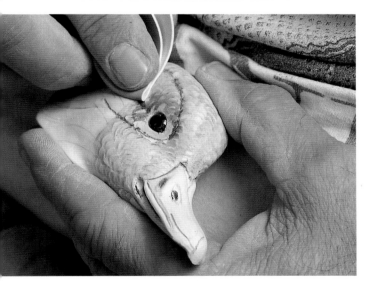

After relieving the feathers of the head, Jim smoothes the area with 400-grit sandpaper. The key word in this process is *subtle.* The feathers should have some definition, but they should not be prominent or have a shingled or fish-scale look.

Jim now uses a pencil to reestablish the location of the feathers. It is important to maintain the distinct margins of the feathers, because individual barbs will later be added to each feather.

A small, thin disk is used on the grinder to carve the long, hairlike feathers of the crest.

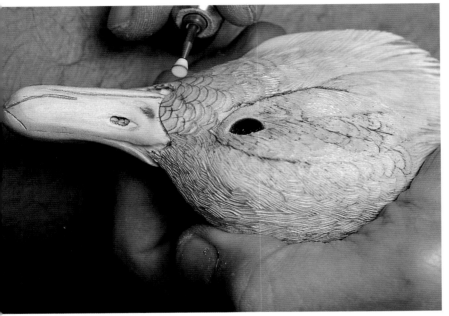

Individual feather barbs are carved with a white inverted stone mounted in the grinder. Jim begins at the base of each feather and works outward. Again, the key word is *subtle*. The small, thin disk shown in the previous photo is used to carve the long, flowing feathers of the crest.

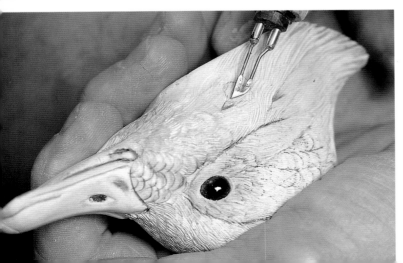

A burning pen could be used for texturing the head, but Jim believes acrylic paints work better when applied over a surface that has been stoned rather than burned. He does use the burning pen at a low temperature to add some accents, such as these little creases between the feathers.

Jim uses texturing techniques as a foundation for painting. For example, because the feathers are somewhat lighter in color near the quill, the dimples carved here will be painted a shade lighter than the surrounding area. Jim will also carve splits in feathers and have feathers of a different color show through.

With the head textured, Jim fits it to the body and draws an outline where it will be mounted. He will use the 2-inch carbide cutter to create a flat surface on which the head will be mounted.

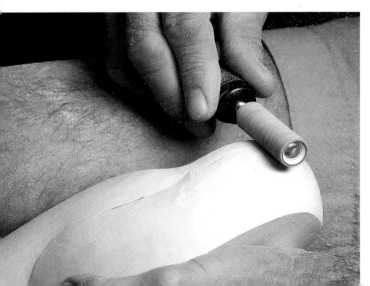

Jim rounds off the breast and then removes wood from the area outlined in pencil. The head should appear tucked into the body.

Jim frequently tries the head for proper fit as he carves. You can change the angle of the head slightly by altering the angle of the shelf on which it will be mounted.

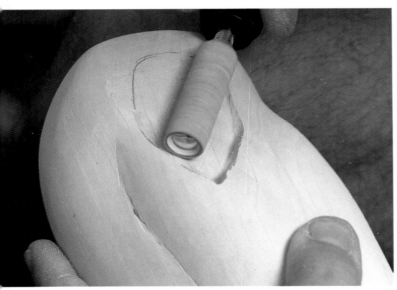

The head should fit into the body rather than be mounted on top of it, so Jim cuts the shelf into the body approximately 1/2 inch at the back of the head.

On a sitting duck like this, with the head tucked in, the neck is actually in front of the breast. Jim will use a grinder to define this area, "pinching in" the breast somewhat to create the look of a neck tucked into the breast feathers.

When Jim is satisfied with the way the head fits, he mixes some two-part epoxy and coats the shelf.

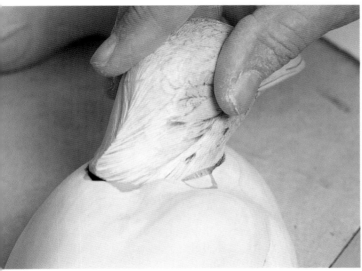

The head is attached. The epoxy is a very strong adhesive, so dowel rods, screws, or other connectors are not needed.

The epoxy hardens quickly, and now Jim is ready to add feather texture to the body. Any gaps where the head meets the body will be filled with Plastic Wood.

CHAPTER NINE

Texturing the Body

Jim will texture the body of the teal much as he did the head, first drawing the feather flow, then sketching individual feathers and relieving them with the grinding tool. He will also carve a few feather splits and some folds in the feathers, and will add individual feather barbs and quills with a stone and burning pen. Again, it's important to study waterfowl anatomy and learn the various feather groups, especially those of the wings.

On this carving, Jim will insert the primary flight feathers rather than carve them from the body of the bird. To do so, he will square off the body behind the secondary and tertial feathers and drill out a cavity into which the feathers will be inserted. Four primary feathers will show on each wing, and they will be inserted after the bird has been painted.

Jim begins this chapter by sketching the feathers with the pencil. Once this is done, they can be relieved with a diamond cutter, a ceramic stone, or a metal ball. "The important thing is to avoid a fish-scale look," says Jim. "The edges should not be sharp; you need only enough definition to provide a hint of a feather. You might also relieve one feather slightly deeper than the next, so that they are irregular, not all the same depth.

"The important thing when texturing, whether you use a stone or burning pen, is to develop a rhythm. It's like playing golf or baseball: You need to warm up and get your rhythm established."

Jim begins by using the pencil to sketch the general feather flow along the side pocket areas.

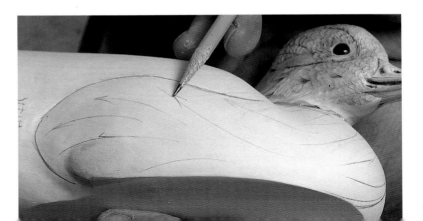

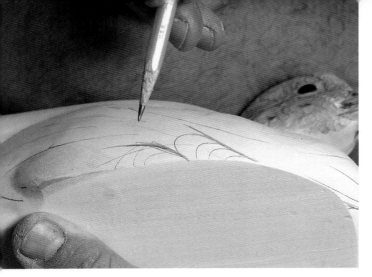

He decides to add a slight curvature in the feathers on the lower breast, as if they had been separated or bent as the teal swam through the water. He adds two smaller separations on the sides of the bird.

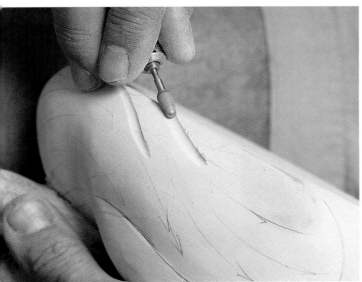

The folds are carved with a diamond cutter on the high-speed grinder. Jim cuts a shallow groove following the pencil line.

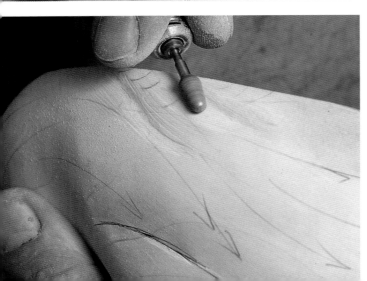

The same tool is used to feather the edge of the grooves, making them more subtle.

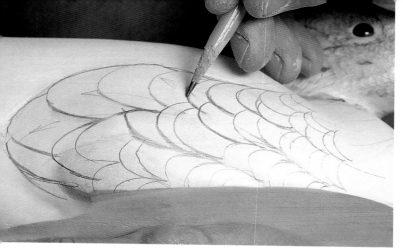

As he did on the head, Jim sketches individual feathers and feather groups with the pencil. He begins with the side pocket areas, first laying out the top row, where the feathers are larger than those of the second row. Below the second row, the feathers generally blend together, with few individual feathers discernible.

The feathers are smaller toward the front of the bird and get larger toward the flanks. The closer to the neck, the smaller the feathers.

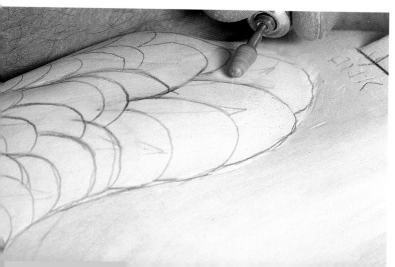

Once the feathers are sketched with a pencil, they can be relieved with a diamond cutter, a ceramic stone, or a metal ball. Jim carves a very shallow groove around each pencil outline.

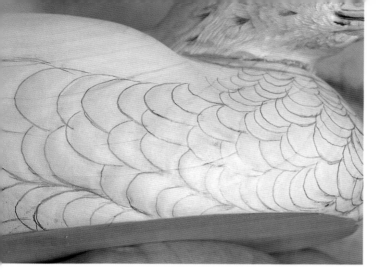

With the side pocket feathers relieved, Jim reestablishes the outline with a pencil.

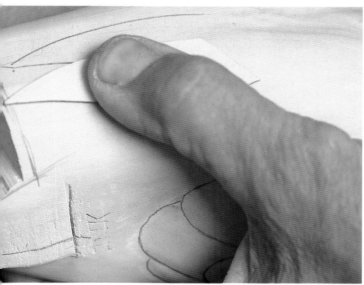

The primary feathers will be inserted, so before carving the other flight feathers, he sketches them and removes the wood behind the secondaries and tertials where the primaries will be inserted. Later, this area will be hollowed out and the primaries inserted and glued into place.

The side pocket feathers have been defined, and now Jim moves to the shoulder area and flight feathers, sketching them with the pencil. Good reference material is needed for this job. A cast study bird, taxidermy mount, or sharp photographs come in handy.

The second tertial feather is the longest, and it ends at a point about 1/4 inch behind where the tail feathers begin. Jim lays this out and, based on the location, establishes the position of the top tertial feather, which is slightly shorter; the third tertial; and then the speculum and the secondaries. Once Jim accurately locates the first feather, using reference material as a guide, the others follow in succession.

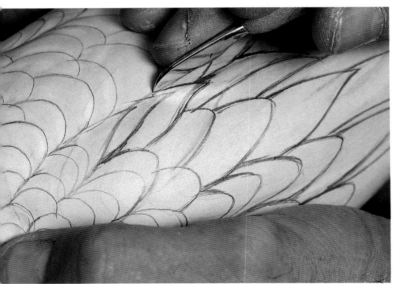

Jim carves the feathers with a knife, cutting around the outline of each, holding the blade perpendicular to the surface of the wood.

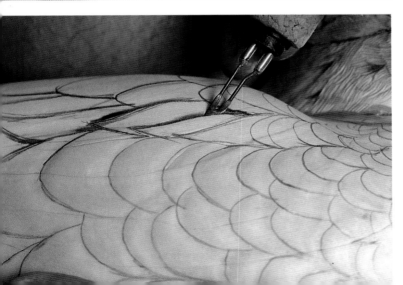

The cuts are then cleaned with a burning pen on a low setting. This cleans and seals the incision, eliminating any rough edges. "The knife gives me control, and when I use the burning pen, I hold it at a slight angle, creating something of a trough. Then I lay the diamond cutter in there, and I get a clean, accurate separation between feathers," Jim says.

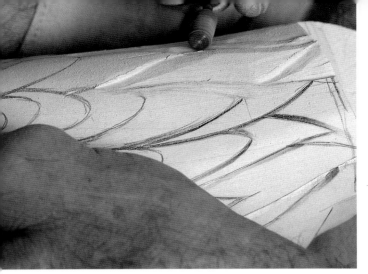

After defining the tertial and scapular feathers, Jim uses a 1/4-inch carbide cutter for a procedure he calls "tenting." Instead of being flat, these feathers have a slightly convex shape, so Jim uses the cutter to reduce the outer edges of the feathers slightly, creating a subtle bend.

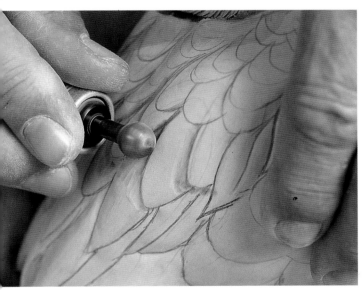

The rounded feathers, like those on the side pockets, are carved with a 1/2-inch ball mounted on the high-speed grinder. The ball is Jim's favorite tool for carving large feathers. It creates a very shallow depression with a gradual edge—just the subtle effect he's looking for.

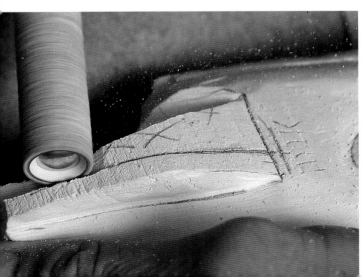

Jim now uses the 2-inch carbide cutter to round off the upper rump, separating it from the tail feathers that extend below it.

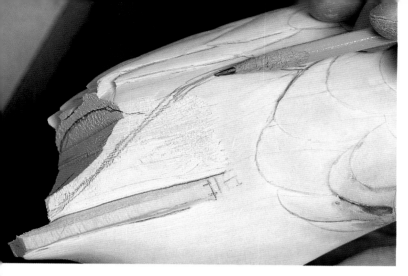

On the study bird, he measures from the tip of the tail to the first row of covert feathers (approximately 1/2 inch). He transfers this measurement to the carved bird and lays out the first row. This defines the margin of the upper rump.

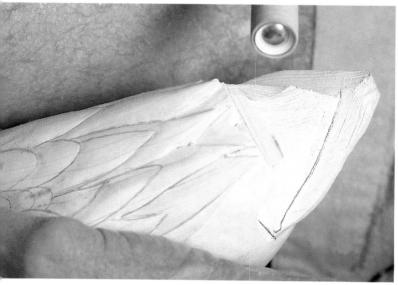

The carbide cutter is used to reduce the rump area, following the line drawn in the previous step. The curved line below the flight feathers indicates the area that will be hollowed out when the primary feathers are inserted.

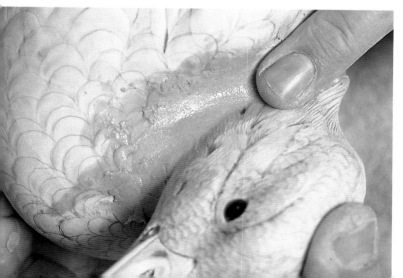

Before doing more texturing on the back and neck area, Jim uses Plastic Wood to seal any openings where the head is mounted on the body. The Plastic Wood, when dry, will texture similarly to wood.

Jim begins texturing under the tail, laying out the puffy feathers with a pencil, adding the vent, and sketching a group of feathers along the flank area.

He uses the 1/2-inch ball to carve along the margins of the sketched feathers as he did on the side pockets.

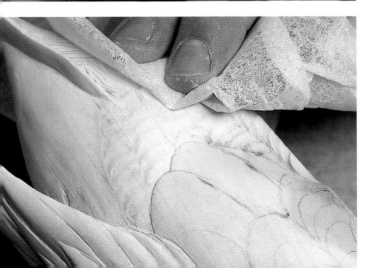

Before adding barbs and quills to the feathers, Jim cleans the wood with a sheet of Bounce, a laundry product designed to reduce static cling. The sheet picks up sanding dust and leaves a smooth surface ideal for texturing.

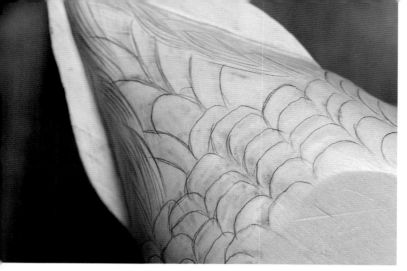

The outlines of the feathers are reestablished with the pencil before texturing. Jim will begin texturing under the rump, then move to the top of the rump, the side pockets, the breast, and the back. Fragile details such as the tail feathers are left for later. He begins under the tail because that area is least often seen, so it gives him a chance to develop his rhythm with the texturing tools in an out-of-the-way place.

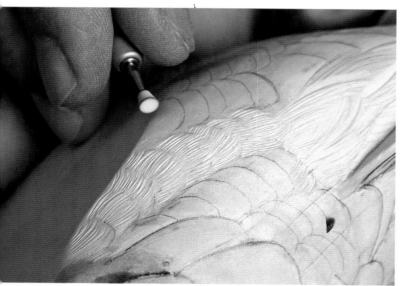

Jim uses various tools during the texturing process. A small white stone is used here to create individual feather barbs on the soft feathers of the flanks. The burning pen also is used a great deal.

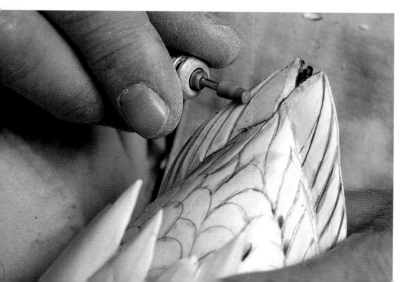

Jim sketches the upper tail covert feathers, cuts along the lines with a knife, and then cleans the cut with the burning pen. The tapered stone is then used to define each feather.

Jim marks the separations between the feathers and transfers these marks under the tail, ensuring that they will be in line. The separations between the feathers are burned under the tail.

Jim carves feather detail with the white stone, then uses the burning pen to scribe a fine line between the stoned lines. This will make them appear to be tighter at the base of the feather, contributing greatly to the illusion of realism.

He makes the feathers appear to overlap by extending texture lines from one feather onto the one next to it. "In teaching classes, I've found that people are challenged by texturing more than perhaps any other aspect of carving except painting," says Jim. "Texturing is a big part of carving, so it's worth learning how to do it properly. It's a very creative process; there are a lot of different things you can do."

Once Jim has textured the tail, he moves to the side pockets. He uses a pencil to sketch lightly the feather flow on the larger feathers. A diamond cutter is used to carve feather detail, following the direction of the pencil lines. A ball on the high-speed grinder smooths the lines left by the diamond, eliminating much sanding.

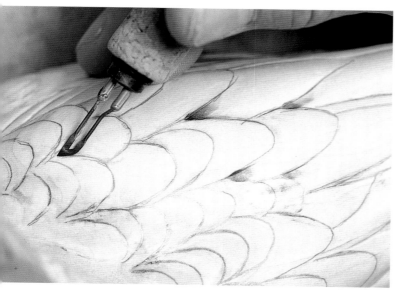

Jim uses the burning pen in some selected areas to add separations or folds between feathers.

Diamond paper or 600-grit sandpaper is used to clean the tip of the burning pen when it gets a buildup of residue. A clean tip is easier to control.

The quills are carved with the burning pen. Jim scribes two parallel lines with the pen, then turns the tip at a slight angle and softens the lines to make the effect less pronounced.

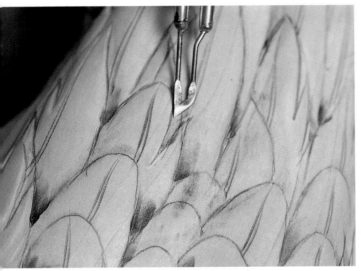

The quills should not stand out, nor should they line up from one feather to the next. Also, each quill does not necessarily have to come to the outside edge of the feather. "Use a low to moderate temperature," Jim says. "The detail will be finer and it will paint better."

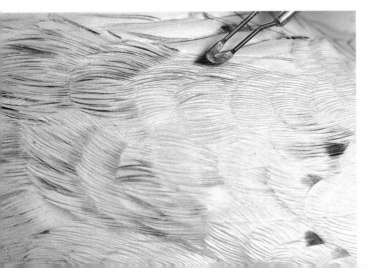

Jim uses the burning pen and diamond cutter to add a few subtle ripples to the feathers, adding to the illusion of softness. He will also carve some splits in the feathers, such as in the tertials where they overlay the green speculum. In this way, the carving again provides a foundation for painting. The tertials are brownish gray, but the green speculum will show through at the split.

CHAPTER TEN

Carving and Inserting the Primary Feathers

Jim is inserting the primary feathers on this teal rather than carving them from the body of the bird. Four primary feathers show on each wing, and Jim uses a paper pattern (see page 18) to trace each feather onto a sheet of basswood or tupelo $1/32$ inch thick. He uses the same patterns for each wing, flipping them over to trace the feathers for the opposite wing.

The primaries are trial-fitted, cut to length, and put together with what Jim considers a proper overlap. Jim then glues them with five-minute epoxy, clips them together in position, and holds them as the glue sets, pinching them slightly to produce a slightly cupped shape.

The primary inserts are fitted into the bird and held in place with pencil erasers. Jim textures them with the burning pen, but he will not glue them in position until after the bird has been painted.

To prepare for insertion of the primaries, Jim undercuts the wood beneath the secondary and tertial feathers. The primaries will be cut and glued together, and then fitted into the body of the bird and glued under the secondaries.

Jim measures his study cast to find the proper length of the primaries. Four feathers will show on each wing.

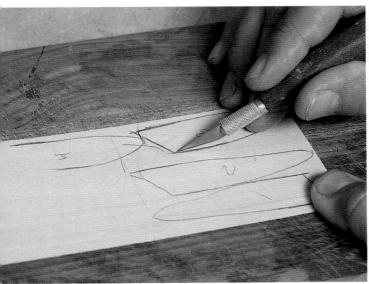

He uses a paper pattern to trace the outline of each onto a thin sheet of basswood. He then flips the four templates over and outlines the four primaries for the other wing. The quill goes on the lateral, or outside, part of the feather. Jim then cuts out the feathers with a knife.

Each feather is sanded with 400-grit paper.

The four feathers are assembled and trial-fitted in the body of the bird.

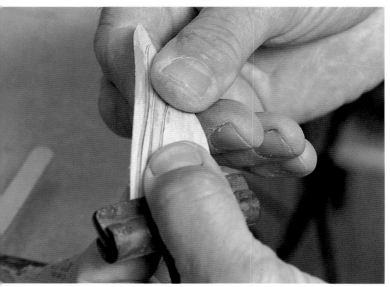

When Jim is happy with the fit, he glues the feathers together with five-minute epoxy, cupping the feathers slightly to produce a subtle curve.

The grinder is used to smooth the edges where the feathers overlap and to thin down the insert.

Once the inserts are carved, they are inserted in the body of the bird and held in place with wedge-shaped pencil erasers. Jim experiments with different angles, deciding on one in which a primary overlaps one of the secondary feathers.

The two inserts have been put in place temporarily. Once they are fitted, Jim will remove them for texturing and painting. They will be epoxied in place when the bird is completed.

This angle shows how the primaries and secondaries fit together. One of the advantages of carving feather inserts is that you can vary the way the feathers overlap, doing things that may be difficult when working with one piece of wood.

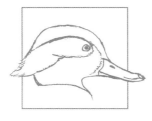

CHAPTER ELEVEN

Painting and Finishing the Teal

Prior to painting, Jim seals the surface of the wood with Teekay's Wood Sealer (Curt's Waterfowl Corner, 123 Leboeuf Street, Montegut, LA 70377). The applications are brushed on, with the sealer being allowed to dry between coats.

Jim uses Jo Sonja paints because they work well with his color-to-water blending technique. The colors he will use to paint the teal are as follows: nimbus gray, Payne's gray, raw umber, burnt umber, raw sienna, burnt sienna, brown earth, carbon black or mars black, phthalo blue, pine green, phthalo green, Hooker's green, yellow oxide, yellow light, titanium white, iridescent white, smoke pearl, and pearl essence powder in green, white, and blue.

He attaches a 2 by 2 keel to the bottom of the carving to make it easier to handle during painting.

Jim begins with two applications of gesso tinted with Payne's gray, nimbus gray, and raw umber. This provides a uniform painting surface for the colors that will follow. The tinted gesso will also serve as a base color in some areas, showing through the vermiculated side pockets, for example.

The colors are put on in very thin washes and are built up through successive applications. Jim often uses a color-to-water blending technique, which produces a soft, gradual edge to a color. He will dampen an area with water, apply the paint, and blend the paint into the water to dilute the color further at its edge.

Since the colors he uses are transparent, he also will create highlights by applying a bright color and then covering it with a darker one. An example of this would be the speculum, which is painted yellow, then covered with green. The result is a green speculum with just a hint of yellow in its center. The effect is subtle but effective.

Jim uses a wide variety of brushes: a 1-inch stiff-bristle brush for applying gesso; a 3/4- or 1-inch synthetic brush for broad washes; a long, thin liner brush in size 1 or 2 for fine detail and reaching tight places; size 2, 4, and 6 blending brushes; and size 3 and 8 round-tips for feather flicking. All brushes are handmade in Germany to Jim's specifications and are sold through his mail-order business, Greenwing Enterprises.

Jim will use an airbrush at times in this demonstration, but you can get similar results with a fiber brush.

Prior to painting, Jim seals the surface of the wood with Teekay's Wood Sealer. The sealer is brushed on, and is allowed to dry between coats.

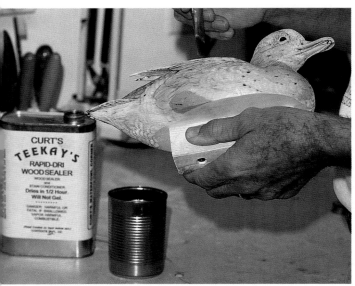

This solution seals the pores of the wood and prepares it for the application of transparent colors. The sealer is brushed on in the direction of the texture lines and is applied in thin coats so that it will not obscure detail.

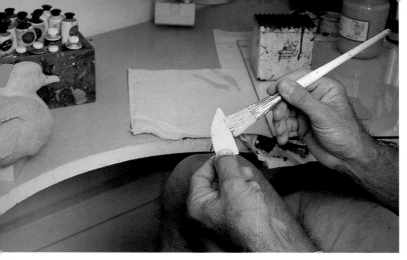

Jim begins with two applications of gesso tinted with Payne's gray, nimbus gray, and raw umber. The mix is 50 percent gesso, 30 percent nimbus gray, and 10 percent each raw umber and Payne's gray. The colors are diluted with water to produce thin washes. Jim adds an equal amount of Jo Sonja flow medium to the water to facilitate blending. Surplus tinted gesso is kept for later use.

Jim puts on a first coat and lets it air dry. Drying with a hair dryer can cause the gesso to shrink slightly, causing pinholes that will be difficult to cover with paint later. Subsequent applications of paint and gesso can be dried with a hair dryer, once this base coat has set up.

When the gesso has dried, Jim adds some feather edges along the side pockets with a cream color mix of 50 percent titanium white, 30 percent raw sienna, 10 percent burnt umber, and 10 percent burnt sienna. The same color is used on the breast of the teal. Jim applies it in a series of very thin washes with a technique called color-to-water blending: He dampens the outline of the breast area with water, then applies the color and blends it into the water, creating a very soft edge.

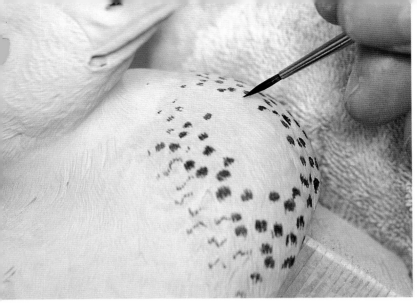

Jim puts three washes on the breast, then paints a series of random black dots on the area. The color is a fifty-fifty mix of carbon black and burnt umber. The same color will be used later for the vermiculated lines that go on the sides and back, so an extra amount is mixed now for later use.

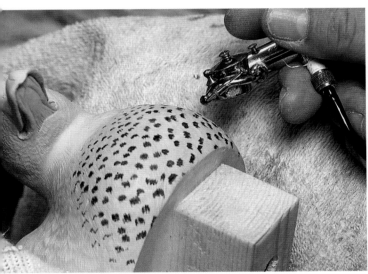

Jim paints the spots first with his Sprankle 10V size 3 vermiculating brush. Then he uses an airbrush to add spots with a softer edge. The spots should be applied randomly and should not be symmetrical. They are larger along the lower breast area and elongated along the sides where they meet the vermiculated side pockets. The neck area also is vermiculated.

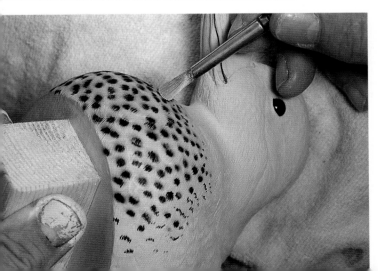

Once the spots are completed, Jim adds feather edges in the manner he did earlier on the side pockets. He uses a curved, feather-flicking brush, with an arc shaped similarly to the feather edge. On the breast, Jim uses the gesso base color mixed earlier, adding to it a small amount of iridescent white and titanium white to provide a subtle sheen.

A #1200 size 1 brush is used to extend some of the white feather edges through the black spots.

The breast is dried with a hair dryer.

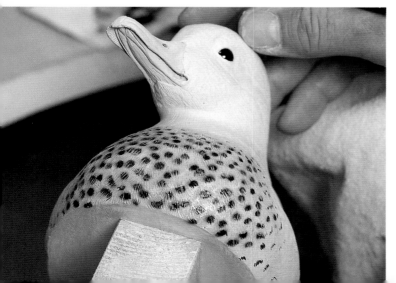

A very thin wash of burnt umber slightly darkens the breast and brings the values closer together. The burnt umber is absorbed into the texture lines, helping to provide definition to the carved detail. This is covered by a wash of diluted matte medium varnish, which gives the breast a slightly waxy look.

Jim paints the head next with Jo Sonja brown earth. He first outlines the eye area where the green will go, and then paints the crown, cheek, and neck with the color.

The key in painting with transparent colors is to build intensity gradually through a series of thin washes. Here the head has had one application of color.

The head has now had three washes, and the intensity is building. A fourth wash will bring the color to the point Jim wants.

After the fourth wash, Jim uses the small lining brush to extend some of the brown onto the neck, creating an irregular edge.

The green head patch is painted next, again by gradually building color. The color is a mixture of 50 percent pine green, 40 percent phthalo green, and 10 percent carbon black. It's not necessary to blend to water and create a soft edge here. The margin is fairly abrupt, and a thin line of cream will later be added around the perimeter of the green.

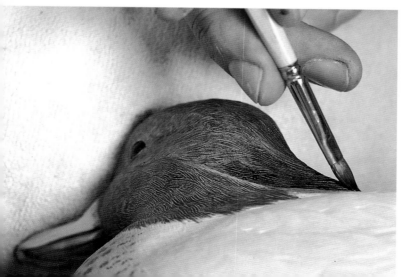

Jim puts on three washes of paint and adds a bit of green pearl essence to add a hint of iridescence.

The outer portions of the green patch are darkened with washes of carbon black and burnt umber, mixed in equal proportions. Jim dampens the inner portion of the green patch with water, applies the color to the outside, and then blends to water to get a gradual transition. An airbrush can also be used for this.

Yellow oxide is used to create very light feather edges in the green patch.

A very thin wash of phthalo blue is applied to the green patch and the crest to add depth and transparency to the green.

Feather detail on the crown is enhanced by edging individual feathers with a buff color made by mixing 60 percent titanium white, 10 percent burnt sienna, and 30 percent burnt umber. Jim uses a small feather-flicking brush to add this color to the feather edges.

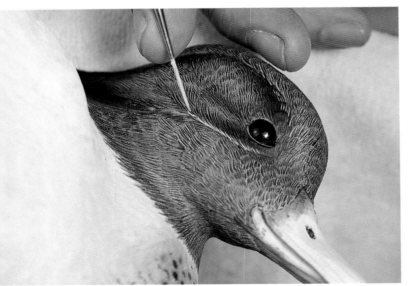

The line that runs around the perimeter of the green patch is a cream color made by mixing 50 percent titanium white, 25 percent yellow oxide, and 25 percent burnt umber. The line is painted with a small brush, with the strokes following the carved feather texture. It is widest under the eyes.

A thin dark line goes behind the bill. Jim uses a mix of equal parts carbon black and burnt umber. It can be applied with either a small brush or airbrush, or a combination of the two.

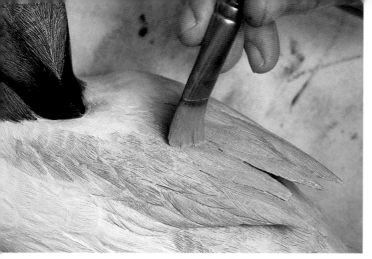

Jim will paint the back next—the tertials, scapulars, and upper rump. He begins by applying several very thin washes of a mix of 45 percent nimbus gray, 25 percent burnt umber, 25 percent raw umber, and 5 percent carbon black. He also adds a little iridescent white to provide a slight gloss.

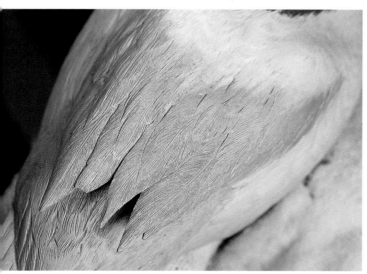

The area gets three thin washes, each dried with the hair dryer between applications. Jim dampens the area above the paint and blends to it, creating a soft edge.

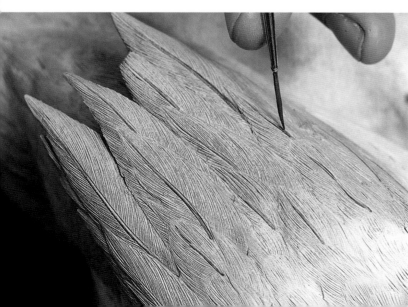

Jim then mixes 55 percent raw umber, 25 percent burnt umber, 15 percent nimbus gray, and 5 percent carbon black and uses this color with a lining brush to paint the quills where they show on the tertial and scapular feathers.

The same mix is used to darken the centers of the back feathers. Jim uses the color-to-water painting technique, dampening the area around where the paint will go, and then blending the color to the water to create a gradual edge.

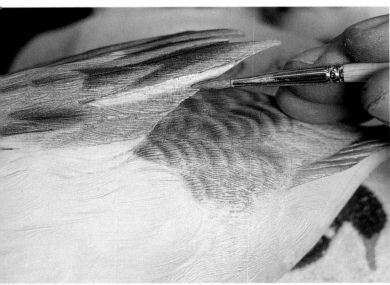

Before painting the speculum, Jim will paint the upper tertial feathers with the white gesso mixture.

Then he will dampen the white, apply black (carbon black and burnt umber in equal parts), and blend it to water.

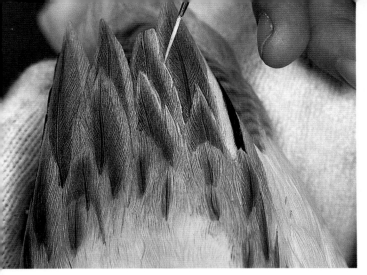

A cream edge is applied to the tertial and scapular feathers. This consists of the gesso mix used earlier, with a little raw umber added to produce the buff color. A small brush is used to create a fine line around the perimeter of the feathers.

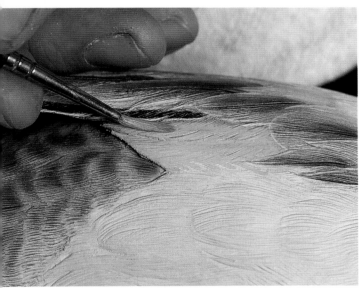

The speculum will be painted green, but first a base coat of yellow will go on. Because acrylic paints are transparent, this will provide highlights under the green washes. Here Jim uses yellow light.

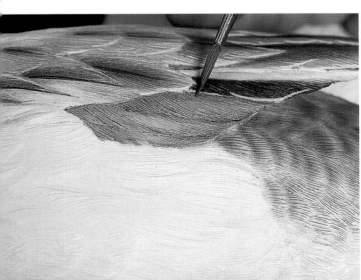

Hooker's green darkened with 10 percent carbon black is painted on the outer margins of the speculum. The center is dampened with water, and the color is blended into it.

A second wash is applied, and then a third one goes over the entire speculum, leaving a yellow highlight in the center. Jim adds a small amount of green pearl essence in the final wash to produce some iridescence.

The rear margins of the speculum are darkened further by black, blended to water. A small amount of blue pearl essence is added to the black. A thin gray line, gesso tinted with 25 percent raw umber, is painted on the trailing edge.

Jim uses the airbrush to paint the primary feather inserts. The primaries and the tail feathers are painted with a mix of 60 percent burnt umber, 30 percent titanium white, 5 percent carbon black, and 5 percent raw sienna. The outer edges of the primaries and tail feathers are darkened by adding a small amount of carbon black and burnt umber to the base color. This can either be airbrushed on or blended to water, as Jim did in previous steps.

Jim uses gesso warmed with 25 percent raw umber to highlight the feather tips behind the tail and on the trailing edges of the primary feathers.

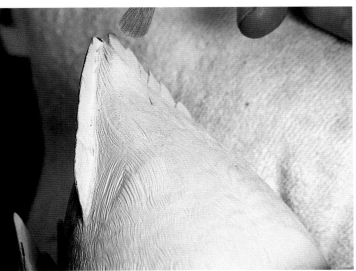

The undertail covert feathers are painted with a mixture of 80 percent gesso, 10 percent burnt umber, and 10 percent yellow oxide, which combine to produce a champagne color.

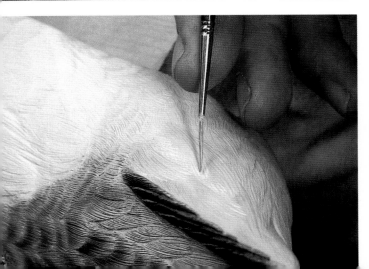

Jim then edges the feathers under the rump with straight raw sienna. This can be done with either a brush, blending to water, or an airbrush. Gesso tinted with 25 percent raw umber is used to highlight some of the feathers under the tail. This step provides three color values in the area: the base color, white, and raw sienna.

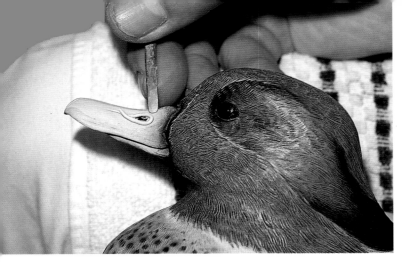

Before painting the bill, Jim will put a membrane around the nostrils. He uses Apoxie Sculpt brand two-part epoxy compound. He rolls out a small string of the material, carefully places it around each nostril, and shapes it with a blunt tool.

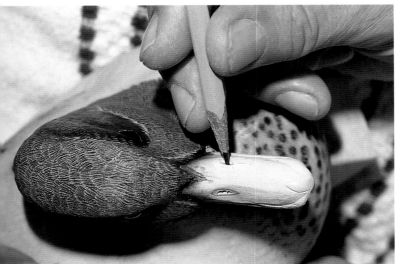

A pencil is used to shape the inner part of each nostril.

The epoxy encircles the nostrils, filling the depression carved when the nostrils were drilled. Apoxie Sculpt can also be used to add a membrane around the eyes or on the bill.

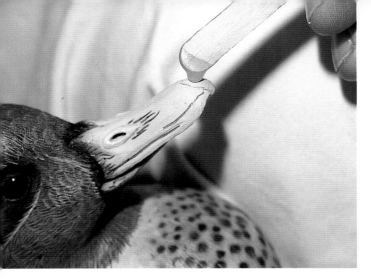

Clear, five-minute epoxy adhesive—the material used to fasten the head to the body—is used on the nail. This adds some strength to a fragile part of the bird.

The bill is now ready for painting. Jim has added a few subtle wrinkles around the nostrils with the point of a pencil.

Jim begins by applying a coat of gesso tinted with about 25 percent raw umber on the lower part of the upper mandible. Either an airbrush or a sable brush could be used for this.

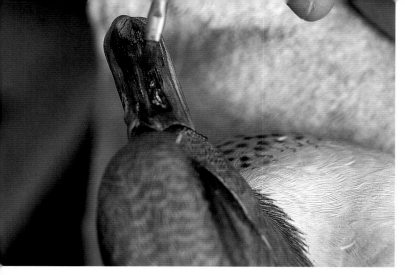

The lower part of the mandible has a brownish cast, with more black on the top of upper mandible. Jim paints this area by first applying straight burnt umber, followed by a wash of burnt umber and carbon black mixed fifty-fifty. These colors are blended to the water along the lower margins of the mandible.

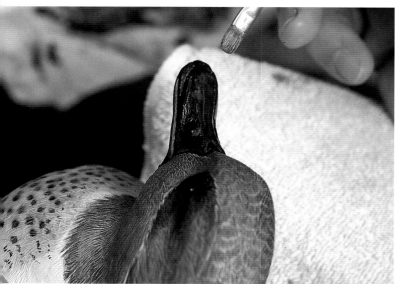

Matte medium-varnish provides a final coat. This gives the bill a leathery look and also affords it some protection.

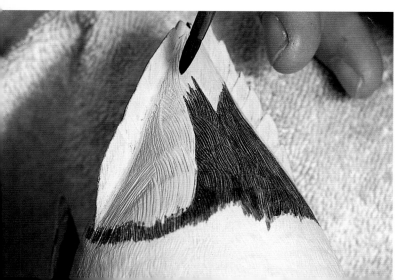

Jim paints the black area under the rump with the fifty-fifty mix of burnt umber and carbon black.

The black also is applied to the lower halves of the first row of tail covert feathers. The top portions of the feathers get the same champagne color used earlier under the rump, a mix of 80 percent gesso, 10 percent yellow oxide, and 10 percent burnt umber.

On the rump area, over the champagne color, Jim adds a series of irregular black dots. He applies them here with the airbrush, but a sable brush could be used.

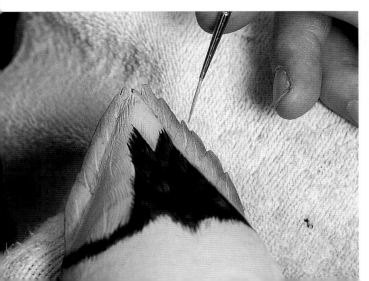

The feathers under the tail are painted with a mix of 80 percent nimbus gray, 10 percent carbon black, and 10 percent burnt umber, with a small amount of iridescent white added. Outside edges are darkened slightly by a thin wash of carbon black. The quills are painted with smoke pearl, using a small lining brush.

Jim now begins the process of vermiculation, painting the many irregular lines that cover the side pockets and part of the neck and back. There are three ways to put on vermiculation: using a sable brush, a pen with a worn felt tip, or a wax pencil. Jim believes that the first method, though more time-consuming, best replicates the vermiculated lines on a live teal. The color is the fifty-fifty mix of carbon black and burnt umber used for the spots on the breast.

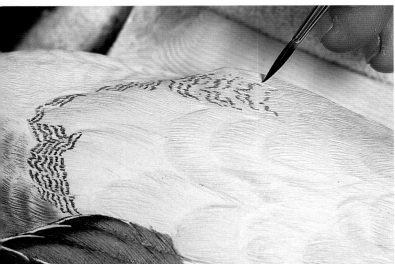

"Vermiculation differs somewhat from bird to bird," Jim says, "so it's important to get good reference. The width and shapes of the lines vary, so study them carefully." Jim often will use some diluted burnt umber to put some feather edges on the side pockets and back before vermiculating, creating a slightly irregular base for the lines.

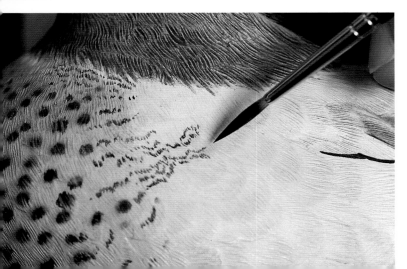

On the breast, the vermiculated lines extend into the area where there are irregular dots. Photographs or taxidermy mounts will show details such as these.

Jim advises keeping a uniform distance between vermiculation lines, and not having them follow the curvature of the feather. "Look at the photographs and see how I've semi-arched the lines, starting at the center of the feather and working from there," he says.

Jim holds his brush perpendicular to the surface of the bird and moves it back and forth vertically, not horizontally, creating short, irregular lines. He does $1/8$ to $1/4$ inch, then stops and leaves a gap before beginning again.

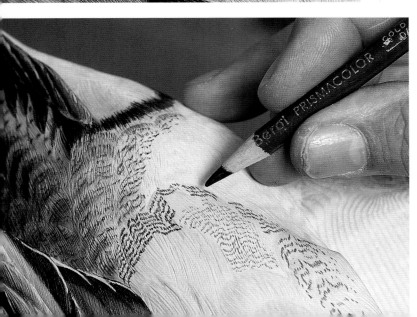

Jim shows here how a Prismacolor pencil can be used. Though this is faster, he prefers the brush because he can vary the width and intensity of the lines. For example, where the vermiculated lines become wider along the belly, Jim presses down a little harder on the brush to get wider lines.

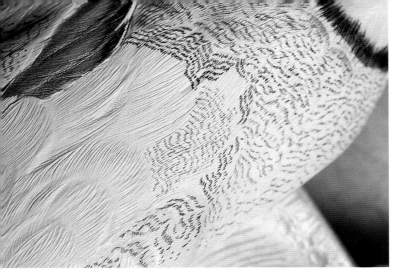

The belly of the bird is much lighter than the sides, as shown here. The color is less intense, and the lines are farther apart.

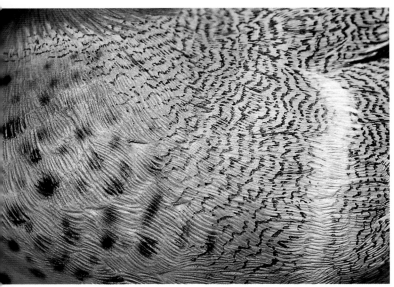

On the sides of the breast, the vermiculation extends into the cream area, but a vertical line forward of the side pockets is left white.

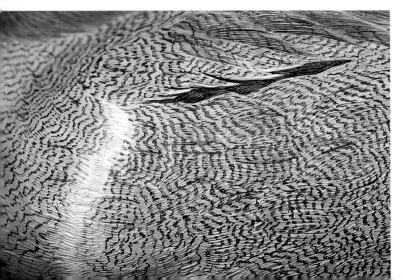

This close-up shows the pattern of vermiculation on the side pocket.

The primary feathers are painted separately from the rest of the bird and are inserted after painting. Two-part epoxy adhesive is used to hold them in place.

Jim Sprankle comments on his finished carving of a green-winged teal: "Here's the finished bird, completely carved and painted. Compare this bird with the reference photos included in chapter 2. Note here the vermiculated lines on the sides and the way in which they join the breast. A close study of reference photos enables you to paint with accuracy in both color and detail."

"This tight shot of the head shows the detail of the feather layout and flow of feathers. Note the whitish markings around eye. They don't follow the green area completely to crest; refer to photo showing rear view of head."

"Notice details of the bill and feather layout directly behind the bill. These small feathers have been relieved with a small white stone before being detailed with a burning pen."

"The rear view of the teal's head, showing how the green area blends into bluish/black area toward the crest. This is a good illustration of white marking around the green area."

"This shows the coloring of the tertials and the secondary feather groupings. Notice the configuration of vermiculation."

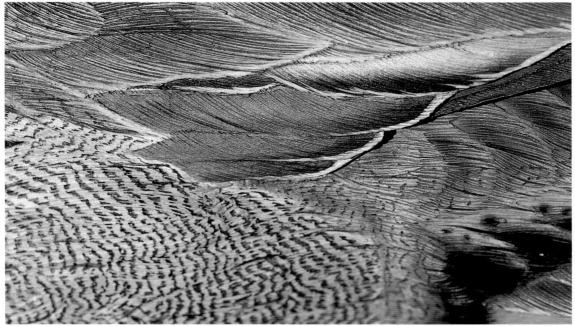

"Note the subtle blending on the tertial feathers."

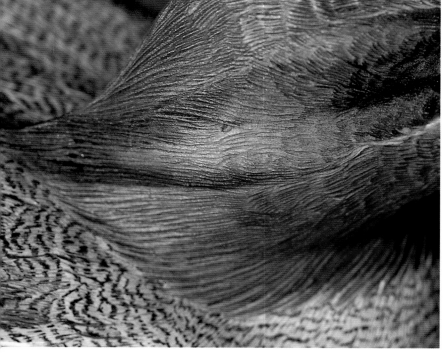

"Look closely at how the small feathers on the head turn into long feathers toward the back of the head and onto the breast. Note also the yellow highlights on the green area."

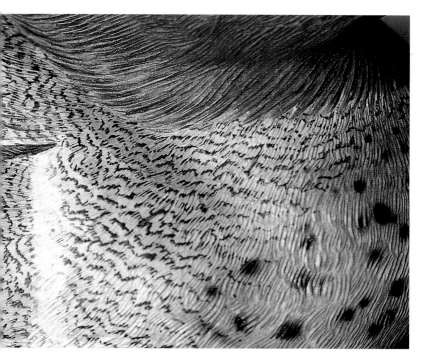

"The transition area between the head and breast is shown in this close-up. Study the vermiculation and how it blends into the spots on breast."

"Pay careful attention to the markings and transition area on the upper rump. Don't forget the faint black spots on the first row of upper tail coverts."

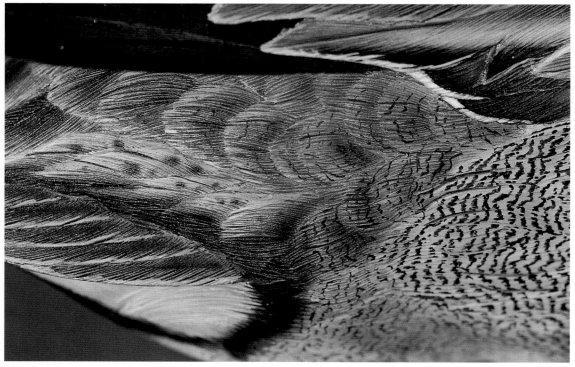

"An interesting close-up of the upper and lower rump areas showing the overlapping of feather texturing on the first row of under-tail covert feathers. I have always referred to this area as the 'champagne area.'"

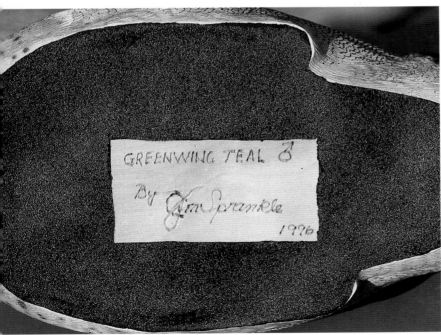

GREENWING TEAL ♂

By Jim Sprankle

1996

"You guessed it! The finishing touch—I sprayed green felt, or flocking, onto an area painted black and I left space to add name and date. Remember, if your name is on your carving, DO THE BEST JOB YOU KNOW HOW TO DO. HAPPY CARVING!"